CONFRONTING THE PREDICAMENT OF BELIEF

The Quest for God in Radical Uncertainty

CONFRONTING THE PREDICAMENT OF BELIEF

The Quest for God in Radical Uncertainty

A Loma Linda Dialogue
with Clayton and Knapp

WIPF & STOCK · Eugene, Oregon

Wipf and Stock Publishers
199 W 8th Ave, Suite 3
Eugene, OR 97401

Confronting the Predicament of Belief
The Quest for God in Radical Uncertainty
By Walters, James W. and Clayton, Philip
Copyright © 2014 by Walters, James W. All rights reserved.
Softcover ISBN-13: 978-1-7252-8360-2
Hardcover ISBN-13: 978-1-7252-8363-3
eBook ISBN-13: 978-1-7252-8362-6
Publication date 6/24/2020
Previously published by CrowdScribed, 2014

This edition is a scanned facsimile of the original edition published in 2014.

CONTENTS

The Origins of this Book vii
Acknowledgments viii
Foreword *by Christopher Southgate* xi

PART I
Critical Reflections on Philip Clayton and Steven Knapp's
The Predicament of Belief: Science, Philosophy, Faith **(Oxford University Press, 2011)**

1. VALID REASONS FOR DOUBTING
   A Reflection on Chapter 1, "Reasons for Doubt"
   Dennis Hokama 3

2. AN ARID FAITH WELL DEFENDED
   A Reflection on Chapter 2, "The Ultimate Reality"
   William Breer 23

3. FROM THEODICY TO ANTHROPODICY
   A Reflection on Chapter 3, "Divine Action and the
   Argument from Neglect"
   Lee F. Greer 37

4. THE ULTIMATE REALITY: WHO AM I TO KNOW?
   A Reflection on Chapter 4, "The Plurality of Religions"
   Ervin Taylor 77

5. WHY I BELIEVE IN THE *BODILY* RESURRECTION
   OF JESUS AND THINK THAT CLAYTON AND
   KNAPP MIGHT TOO
   A Reflection on Chapter 5, "The Scandal of Particularity,
   Part I: The Resurrection Testimony"
   David R. Larson 91

6. NON-REDUCTIVE PHYSICALISM VS. THE
SPECTER OF CLASSICAL DUALISM
A Reflection on Chapter 6, "The Scandal of
Particularity, Part II: Jesus and the Ultimate Reality"
Calvin Thomsen 109

7. PRIVATE EVIDENCE AND RESPONSIBLE BELIEF
A Reflection on Chapter 7, "Doubt and Belief"
Richard Rice 125

8. STRICTLY RATIONAL BELIEF MISSES THE GENIUS
OF RELIGION
A Reflection on Chapter 8, "The Spectrum of Belief
and the Question of the Church"
James W. Walters 141

PART II
A Response to Our Critics

Philip Clayton
Steven Knapp

INTRODUCTION 161

9. PARTICIPATION AND EMERGENCE 165
10. CHRIST AS "RISEN" 179
11. WHAT STANCE DO I TAKE TOWARD MY
    OWN BELIEFS? 193
12. EPILOGUE: SEEKING BELIEF AND COMMUNITY
    IN AN AGE OF DOUBT 215

Contributors... 221

ON THE ORIGINS OF THIS BOOK

The origin of this book is a theologically moderate to liberal Sabbath School class at Loma Linda University (LLU)—a Seventh-day Adventist entity.

Significantly, LLU embodies twin aspects of Adventism—education and health care—which compel it to confront mainstream culture. LLU has thousands of students earning advanced degrees, and many more employees who encounter hundreds of thousands of patients each year. It would be unusual if the juxtaposition of higher education and gaping human need didn't result in significant probing of life's big questions.

The class, having begun in the mid-1970s, has a membership of 30 to 40, mostly professional people coming from such fields as medicine, law, theology, psychotherapy, the natural and social sciences, and literature. The most common theme is science and religion, but there is also great variety as illustrated by these authors who have visited over the years: John B. Cobb, Jr., Langdon Gilkey, James M. Robinson, Hugh Ross, Michael Shermer, Huston Smith, and John Howard Yoder.

The Predicament of Belief: Science, Philosophy, Faith was co-authored by Philip Clayton and Steven Knapp and published by Oxford University Press in 2011. Critiques of its eight chapters were originally presented in weekly class sessions spanning April through June 2012, with half of the presentations by class members and half by LLU religion professors. To conclude the *Predicament* discussion, Professor Clayton attended the class and orally responded to the written critiques he had earlier received. Subsequently, Walters broached the idea of possible publication of the dialogue, and this book is the result.

ACKNOWLEDGMENTS

Books come in various forms, but this one is particularly unusual in that it's primarily a chapter-by-chapter critique by eight diverse persons of an earlier book whose two authors then constructively utilize those criticisms to pare, refine and further their original argument—all in pursuit of Christian truth in challenging times.

This book is the result of the happy coincidence of an interested religious study group and a willing Christian thinker. In 2012, Loma Linda's Sabbath Seminars, a lay group that meets weekly, chose to discuss Philip Clayton and Steven Knapp's *The Predicament of Belief: Science, Philosophy, Faith,* and Clayton agreed to visit the group and respond to his readers. Now, two years later, due to dedicated individuals, this work has emerged.

Of course, this volume would not exist except for that exceptional group of eclectic seekers (see The Origins of this Book) who chose to study *The Predicament of Belief*. The class members' reactions to the book's argument varied as widely as their social and spiritual journeys. Regardless, without this lay group's desire to grapple with the most pressing issues of Christian faith, the book you are now holding would not exist.

Equally obvious is the fact that this "reactive" volume would not exist without that which provoked it—*The Predicament of Belief*. In their book, Clayton and Knapp do not just acknowledge but also powerfully articulate the challenge to traditional Christian belief posed by contemporary science, theodicy, biblical criticism, and multiple religious traditions. And further, they welcome the intellectual/cultural progress that produces those challenges, believing that Christian faith must and can incorporate today's knowledge—resulting in their truly integrative model of faith. Clayton and Knapp's receptive response to their critics, as seen in Part II of this volume, only underscores their openness to refinement of their progressive faith.

The authors of the critical essays in this present volume originally wrote their pieces as parts of a local study group's ongoing life. Later the idea of publication hatched, and then they had opportunity to refine their analytical arguments. The authors vary widely in ideological commitments, personality types, and religious interests, but they share a dedication to open pursuit of Christian truth and are willing to think intensely toward that end.

A number of talented individuals have made this book possible through overall design and editing of manuscripts: Brianne Donaldson, Justin Heinzekehr, Gayle Foster, Alice Kong, and Jondelle McGhee.

It has been a joy to personally work with Philip Clayton and Steven Knapp on this book, as well as to co-host the Sabbath Seminars that Clayton has visited on four different occasions. Given Clayton's challenging professorial duties at Claremont School of Theology and Claremont Graduate University, and given Steven Knapp's heavy responsibilities as president of George Washington University, it is remarkable that they would take so seriously the essays by myself and my colleagues, but it is in character with their desire to get beyond esoteric theorizing to dialogue with a thoughtful lay public, as achieved in the Sabbath Seminars class project.

Finally, I would like to dedicate this volume to the dean of the School of Religion at Loma Linda University, Jon Paulien. Dean Paulien came to LLU from the Adventist church's primary theological seminary, Andrews University, Berrien Springs, Michigan, eight years ago and encountered a different religious atmosphere at Loma Linda than he had at Andrews where he received his doctorate in New Testament and taught for some 25 years. In an over-simplification Dean Paulien sees Andrews as serving the Adventist church and its internal needs, whereas he sees Loma Linda meeting different needs as it interfaces with the broader society. He would see this present book, which he approves of (not to say agrees with), as part of LLU's contribution to the later emphasis.

Jim Walters

~

We thank Guy Reifenberg and Kokopeli Adventure tours (kokopeliadventures.com) for permission to use the cover image. Above all, we wish to thank the members of Loma Linda's Sabbath Seminars, and especially the chair, Jim Walters, for their thoughtful attention to the arguments in our previous book and for their willingness to engage in an open dialogue on a very challenging set of issues. We are also grateful for their hospitality during Philip Clayton's four trips to Loma Linda (and counting). Each trip brought probing questions from men and women who think deeply about their faith and the changing face of religion in the contemporary world. Without this sort of willingness to follow the questions wherever they lead, Christianity will not be able to remain relevant to a rapidly evolving world.

Finally, we warmly thank artist Lee Greer II for his three gifts on behalf of the class: beautiful oil paintings of storm-tossed sailing ships, which have come to symbolize the journey of faith.

Philip Clayton and Steven Knapp

~

FOREWARD

The Predicament of Belief is one of the most important explorations of theology in the light of science to have emerged in recent years. I am delighted to write a Foreword to this very creative dialogue between the eight critics from Loma Linda and the authors of *Predicament*, Philip Clayton and Steven Knapp.

I first encountered this material in 2005, in the beautiful surroundings of the Pope's summer palace at Castel Gandolfo. Clayton and Knapp presented arguments on divine action to a colloquium co-sponsored by the Vatican Observatory and the Center for Theology and the Natural Sciences at Berkeley. They engaged in a vigorous and very creative dialogue there with Wesley Wildman, author of "the Argument from Neglect." The colloquium later featured in Mark Dowd's award-winning documentary "Where was God in the Tsunami?" This dialogue with Wildman also featured in an enthralling exchange at the American Academy of Religion in 2010.

One of the most remarkable features of the Clayton-Knapp partnership is that they have written this important book while holding senior positions in the governance of important universities on opposite sides of the U.S. Their partnership is a model of how important collaboration can be in theology, a salutary lesson for those who are inclined to insist on working alone. I suspect too that collaboration makes theologians more open to the sort of critical challenge we see in this present book, since always ideas are being formed and fused in the crucible of dialogue.

It is in engagement with the hardest questions that the science-theology conversation really bites, and Clayton and Knapp face full-on the problem of divine providential action in light of the evils of which the world is full. They also respond to another huge challenge to Christian truth-claims—that of the durability of the truth-claims of ancient confessions very different from the Christian.

Dennis Hokama is the first of the Loma Linda critics to offer a critique of *The Predicament of Belief*. He opens this present book by considering the problem of doubt, and of the "Christian minimalism" that Clayton and Knapp advocate, with its lowered standard for truth-claims about a "not-less-than-personal" divine reality. He takes

Clayton and Knapp to task for their approach to epistemology, and (strikingly) what he sees as their over-optimistic assessment of Christian truth-claims—given the history of the Christian tradition and recent work on the historical Jesus.

William Breer gives his critique the provocative title "An Arid Faith Well Defended." He contends that Clayton and Knapp are in fact talking to "a small and specialist audience" of scientifically-informed intellectuals wanting to cling to "some (or a few) of the historical tenets of Christianity." He suggests other ways forward.

Ervin Taylor tackles the question of the plurality of religions, recognizing that this is indeed a major reason for doubting the truth-claims of any one faith. He then tackles in detail the question of what "personal" means in the description of ultimate reality as not-less-than-personal.

I have myself written in the areas of theodicy and divine action, for example in *The Groaning of Creation: God, Evolution, and the Problem of Evil* (Westminster John Knox Press, 2008). I am particularly interested in the way the divine action debate has shifted from the mechanistic preoccupations of the end of the 20th Century to a more moral treatment of the problem with providence. Readers who share my interest will read with particular fascination Lee F. Greer's critique of Chapter 3 of *The Predicament of Belief*. Greer deploys considerable knowledge of the eighteenth-century arguments on theodicy, and argues with forensic skill against Clayton and Knapp's "not even once" argument against divine intervention, and also against their "anomalous monism." The latter makes space for divine encouragement and lure and, according to Clayton and Knapp, evades the critique they level at divine intervention.

I side with Greer on the issue of anomalous monism. I think he is quite right to point out that just as the most refined software still depends on physical electronics, so the most intricate mental functioning still, necessarily, runs on physical substrates, and for God to interact with the human mind is for God to interact with the physical world in just the way Clayton and Knapp find so difficult. However I am inclined to side with the authors of *The Predicament of Belief* on the "not even once" principle. The moral charge against God is greatly increased by particular selective interventions, though Greer is also right that a moral charge exists against the Creator of a suffering-filled world even if that being does not go on to intervene in that world.

Much depends, in this as in other areas, on what is being attempted in theodicy. Greer I think is looking for an argument of such philosophical rigor that a non-believer would have to be convinced, the sort of logical demonstration that—for example—Richard Swinburne has attempted. Clayton and Knapp, rather, are searching for plausibility within a community of inquiry consisting of those of Christian faith (however doubt-laden that faith might be).

Perhaps the section of *The Predicament of Belief* that the orthodox Christian believer will find most difficult is the Clayton-Knapp account of the Resurrection. In keeping with their general view that things happen according to the regularities described by science, and that it is highly problematic to think of God setting aside those regularities in a miraculous way, Clayton and Knapp deny the bodily resurrection of Jesus as ordinarily understood. They set out instead a very sophisticated account of that resurrection, based on the theologies of Paul and the Fourth Gospel. God's Spirit, on this account, is the "substrate" on which the identity of the risen Jesus is implemented, just as his human body had been before his death.

David R. Larson examines this conviction that Christ's risen presence, "personal not physical," could therefore be encountered by believers, without this requiring the setting aside of natural laws. He himself is attracted to the concept of "objective immortality"—that it is enough to believe that "we all survive death as objects in God's memory." Calvin Thomsen considers whether Clayton and Knapp's line of thinking escapes the taint of substance dualism. Richard Rice returns to the theme of doubt, and what might constitute responsible belief.

The Loma Linda critique ends with a chapter by co-editor James W. Walters, considering Clayton and Knapp's views on how church should work in the contemporary context. Walters, rightly in my view, questions the extent to which a "Wittgensteinian game of demonstrating how cold logic can conclude a not-less-than-personal God" can capture what is most important about Christian life in community. He draws on Martin Buber's emphasis not on belief but on trust; his other allies are Stephen Toulmin and David Tracy. Walters thinks Clayton and Knapp miss "an existential level at which we live." We do not operate religiously by believing on the basis of demonstrable evidence (or yet by constantly pondering its plausibility). Ultimately Walters leaves open the question of what understanding of church best suits this secular age. I am delighted to discover from Clayton and Knapp's response that further exploration of ideas of church will be their next big project. There is need for much more development here, in particular I believe in the area of worship, and whether worship changes our understanding of ultimate reality.

Clayton and Knapp respond with their usual graciousness and lucidity to these critiques, in three main sections: participation and emergence, resurrection, and the nature of belief. I think this highly stimulating dialogue draws out clearly that indeed the nub of *The Predicament of Belief* is the authors' position on divine action. One of their key contributions is to map the territory of the range of positions that can plausibly be held in this area of theology, and to recognise that believers, very often, hold a range of positions in different contexts. I was left wondering whether Clayton and Knapp's sense that divine action always involves both the activity of God and the responsive activity of another conscious agent might not have a link with the formulations that Niels Gregersen is developing of "deep incarnation." But that, perhaps, is for a yet further volume.

It is fascinating that several of the Loma Linda faculty, despite teaching within a "conservative" denomination, Seventh-day Adventism, actually want to encourage Clayton and Knapp to be yet more radical. This reinforces just what a special place *The Predicament of Belief* occupies in the spectrum of theological positions. It is unswervingly honest about the challenges that Christian explorers face, challenges that lead many theologians to part company with any realist attempt to say anything about the character of ultimate reality, and others (like Wildman) to deny the personal character, and the benevolence, of that reality. Yet it is equally searching in anatomizing the refuges theistic believers find themselves in when facing the challenges to contemporary faith.

This present book provides an excellent model of what genuinely open, exploratory theological scholarship makes possible. A book like *Confronting the Predicament of Belief: The Quest for God in Radical Uncertainty* should be the beginning, not the end, of a conversation between explorers. What the Loma Linda critics have made possible is a very significant exchange, which in turn has moved the original authors on. I commend both this book, and the process of inquiry it represents, most highly, and hope it will serve as a model for future theological engagement.

Christopher Southgate
University of Exeter, UK

PART I
CRITICAL REFLECTIONS ON *THE PREDICAMENT OF BELIEF:* *SCIENCE , PHILOSOPHY, FAITH*

1

VALID REASONS FOR DOUBTING

A Reflection on Chapter 1, "Reasons for Doubt"

Dennis Hokama

> It is wrong always, everywhere, and for anyone, to believe anything upon insufficient evidence.
> —William K. Clifford, "The Ethics of Belief," 1877

In thinking over Clifford's statement recently, I suddenly realized that we necessarily abide by that dictum, provided that we understand "evidence" in the broader sense, as Richard Rice defines it.[1] Clifford, of course, had only scientific evidence in mind when he wrote the above. But Rice understands evidence as belonging in two categories: public evidence (sensory evidence that is demanded by science), and private evidence (our own customized internal standard of truth based on non-sensory impressions), which ultimately judges public evidence. When our customized standard of private evidence is insufficient for a belief, then we must doubt and cannot believe, though the heavens fall. Each generation, and every individual, calibrates one's own private evidence based on his or her own actual (as opposed to formal) education and experience, or so I will argue. What is generally judged credible evidence for a hypothesis in one generation becomes incredible in another generation or era, though we all have our own customized version of it.

A thought experiment will prove this is true. Suppose that someone offers you a billion dollars to temporarily (let us say for one minute) believe that the earth is flat, such that we could fall off the edge of it. Since it is only temporary, it would not do us any significant damage. Can you re-calibrate your mind temporarily so you can pocket that billion dollars? The answer is no. This is because the "flat earth" hypothesis in the modern era is what William James called a "dead hypothesis" in his famous response to Clifford.[2]

It is this phenomenon of our generational shifting standard of private evidence, in contrast with the relatively permanent religious beliefs, that creates the "predicament of belief" that Philip Clayton and Steven Knapp (hereafter CK) address in their book. The implication of a divine "revelation" that coincides with beliefs of an era, but which becomes obsolete (or dies) as that generation or era passes, is that its actual source was human rather than divine. Legitimizing that shift in belief, while avoiding the parsimonious conclusion, is the heart of that predicament, as I see it.

Seventh-day Adventists, more than almost all other denominations, are in a pickle of a predicament when it comes to belief. For on the one hand, Adventists are among the more conservative of Christians, committed to believing in ancient doctrines like the imminent second coming (Fundamental Belief #25) and a literal six-day creation week less than ten thousand years ago (Fundamental Belief #6). On the other hand, they believe that modern evidence-based medicine is to be the "right arm" of their ministry.

Loma Linda University's medical school is the denomination's flagship professional program, followed by all of its state-accredited

Adventist feeder universities that require the teaching of evolutionary theory in their undergraduate biology programs. Compartmentalized thinking, double talk, schizophrenia, hypocrisy and Sabbath schools that endlessly discuss how to integrate the religion-science divide are exactly what should be expected. With the recent (2010) election of super-conservative General Conference President Ted Wilson, who swore to fight historical-critical interpretation of the Bible in the denomination's universities, the heat on the "predicament of belief" has been cranked up. More than ever, this phrase describes the psychological state of many of its thoughtful members.

Philip Clayton is no stranger to the Sabbath Seminars class and was its guest speaker twice in 2010 alone. When Fritz Guy presented to the Seminars on July 31, 2010, he spoke of talking with Clayton in England about the latter's presentation to the Sabbath Seminars class. Guy reported that Clayton said our class was the "most intelligent lay group" with whom he had ever met.[3]

On the occasion of his second presentation in 2010, I picked up Clayton in Claremont and drove him to class and back home after potluck. While we were discussing various topics as I drove, Clayton spotted my book by Earl Doherty, *Jesus: Neither God nor Man*, picked it up and thumbed through it. That started a discussion on the problems associated with the historicity of Jesus that continued until I dropped him off at his house. He seemed extremely interested, especially in the problems with Galatians 1 and their seeming incompatibility with words attributed to Jesus in Acts 9, 22 and 26.

I will begin with a summary of each section, sometimes explicitly adding my opinion in the commentary and endnotes. My most considered response to this chapter is in my summary notes that conclude the paper.

The Preface

Though at first glance there seem to be many books that already have attempted to resolve doubts about the Christian faith, CK argue that most only do *half* the job.[4] That is, they are only too willing to jettison traditional beliefs as untenable and substitute alternative values. The half that is not done is to address what CK call the "predicament of religious belief in today's world." This predicament, according to CK, has two facets: "Formulating traditional claims about what is ultimately the case in ways that take full account of all the reasons for doubting those claims," and doing "justice to the axiological and theoretical power of those accounts of ultimate reality that metaphysical reflection and religious traditions variously suggest" (8).

Chapter 1 deals with the first facet: the most serious arguments for doubting either religious claims in general or Christian claims in particular. CK admit that their book will not appeal to the fundamentalists in either warring camp; it is only for those who wish to go where reason and experience may lead.

The Christian Hypothesis

What is ontological truth?[5] Where did the universe come from, and does it have any destination? Is there a single reality that can encompass the source and its destination? If such a source exists, does it care at all about humans, the way they live, collectively and individually, during the brief spark of their existence?

All civilizations, say CK, have attempted to answer these ultimate, or ontological questions, and despite the differences in their various claims and theories, the fact that they all attempted to do this is one of the salient artifacts of human culture. According to CK, the "Christian hypothesis" regarding these questions is as follows:

> Christian tradition rests upon a provocative hypothesis about the nature of the universe and its ultimate source. That hypothesis can be restated as the belief or wager that behind or beyond all things, at the beginning of everything we see and know, there exists an ultimate reality that in some sense intended us (or beings like us) to be here and—again in some sense—desires our flourishing. Moreover, that ultimate reality has actually conveyed its intentions to human beings, whether directly or indirectly, and has done so in part through its extraordinary involvement in a particular set of events[6] in human history. (2)

Strategies to Extricate Christianity from its Modern Predicament

First, things have not changed as much as they appear. Second, changes are real, but illegitimate, and must be rejected by those who hold onto the true faith. Third, the changes are vast and legitimate but do not affect the core beliefs on which the religion depends. Fourth, changes are real, but we can save the core beliefs by reinterpreting them, giving them a modern or postmodern interpretation that will enable them to thrive in this new intellectual environment. [7]

CK appear to favor the third option. That is, they "belong to a growing body of people who are committed, or at least strongly drawn, to the ancient claims but who are also deeply struck by evidence and arguments that point in the opposite direction" (3). They also "remain committed to the core Christian hypothesis, despite all the sources of doubt" (4).

These authors recognize that many persons see a widening gap between general philosophical/religions claims about reality and particular religious communities' claims. The former, according to CK, are regarded as rational and academic, but the latter are more cultural, personal, and hardly deserve to be considered a truth claim. One of the central tasks of this book, say CK, "will be to underscore the sharp contrast between these two types of claims and to offer a convincing account of their relationship."

CK distinguish their approach to a defense of Christianity from what they see as problematic "immunization" strategies. What could be wrong with immunization strategies? According to CK, such strategies immunize sectarian doctrine from the incursion of truth about the world, and settle for merely trying to preserve their sectarian tradition. These are immunizing apologetic strategies that CK reject: first, faith should step in where reason fails; second, religious feeling or religious "experience" is more fundamental than reason; third, the richness of Christian "symbols" is sufficient to motivate Christian practice; and fourth, Christian agnosticism, which is content to act on dubious Christian claims, is actually true (4).[8]

For Christians who really want to know the truth, say CK, there is only one alternative: "to understand the reasons for doubt as fully and clearly as possible: to look those reasons, so to speak, directly in the eye" (5). First they consider science.

Science

CK rate the success of scientific explanation as the main reason that people no longer feel compelled to explain their existence in terms of an ultimate reality that is greater, or more important than, the reality of the natural world. CK chart the incredible achievements of science, citing the optimism of some that within the next few decades science may even understand the underlying mechanisms for human consciousness—which Conor Cunningham in *Darwin's Pious Idea* declared inherently impossible.[9] The upshot of such spectacular success has been a growing confidence that it is only a matter of time before all such ancient mysteries will yield to the inevitable advance of science. Methodologically, this presupposes that the world can be explained by natural causes within a closed system. CK call this view the "presumption of naturalism."

CK cite David Hume as the philosopher who articulated the idea that the "presumption of naturalism" was strictly a methodological human rule, and not a metaphysical law.[10] CK state that it is very important that we always make this distinction lest we arbitrarily impose naturalism on the universe.

But CK warn that it is a mistake for religious thinkers to jump from the recognition that methodological naturalism cannot rule out the possibility of miracles to the conclusion that science leaves a traditional belief in miracles untouched. That is a mistake, they say, for two reasons: first, it underestimates the effect of scientific questioning on the traditional tendency to invoke a miracle when something extra-ordinary happens,[11] and second, it prevents those who accept it from asking themselves why the universe should be such that it lends itself so readily to scientific explanation.

Evil and Religious Plurality

The problem of evil is probably the best-known objection to the existence of a good, powerful, loving God. CK articulate the problem of reconciling the hypothesis of a good and powerful God with the existence of bad things: if this God really exists, this being would be expected to stop or prevent evil.

CK cite three examples of horrible things that befall people, including the classic example, the Nazi Holocaust. "Obviously," say CK, "anyone who wishes to argue that the reasons for Christian commitment override the reasons for doubt must give some account of why it is possible, in a God-created universe, for events like these to occur" (9).[12]

CK call the plurality of religions the "most obvious, and one of the most ancient, of all reasons for doubting the claims of

Christianity" (9): other faith traditions that proclaim different things make equally strong claims about the nature and purposes of the ultimate reality, and their adherents are at least as strongly committed to them as Christians are to theirs.

The obvious question is that if other people believe God told them different things, why should we think our religion is superior or a better reflection of God's will than other successful world religions? Isn't it more parsimonious to conclude that any particular religion, including ours, is a human product of a given culture?

If Christian claims are true, why should multiple religions exist in the first place? How could such a powerful and wise personal God, who desires communion with God's own creatures, allow the divine message to be so badly bungled that chaos exists and wars are fought over what God really wants humans to believe and do? If Christianity is true, how could God allow its relations with Judaism to be so savage and horrible over the millennia? Is not this better explained by purely naturalistic "sibling" rivalry?

The State of the Historical Evidence

The previous problem (plurality of religions) shades into the next one. It is bad enough that multiple religions have rival claims as to God's will, but when it comes to Christianity, the problem becomes even more acute. For, according to CK, "Christianity claims that God has acted to communicate God's nature and purposes with humanity in a uniquely clear and powerful way in the events associated with the life and death of a certain Jewish teacher or rabbi in the ancient Roman province of Palestine" (11).

But the only records we have of the way that rabbi was remembered and understood by his followers show no obvious signs that supernatural care was taken to ensure their clarity. For example: first, "none of the records that have come down to us was directly produced by anyone who actually knew...Jesus of Nazareth, during his earthly life," and second, "the records themselves differ in striking ways both in the events they recount and the interpretations they place on those events. Three of those records, the Gospels according to Matthew, Mark, and Luke, are called the 'Synoptic Gospels'... But even those three Gospels—let alone the fourth, the Gospel According to John, which orders events in starkly different ways from the other three—disagree sharply among themselves" (11). CK then go over the number of contradictions in the four gospels in just the crucifixion and its immediate aftermath.[13]

A "chain of custody" is basic to protecting the integrity of evidence. Such a chain is hopelessly and notoriously lacking in all the documents that make up the New Testament, because they all passed through the hands of partisans with strongly vested interests in how the stories were told and interpreted. (Even after the manuscripts arrived in final manuscript form, they had to be recopied every generation by scribes with partisan interests.) The earliest documents we have date to more than a century after the time of Jesus.

The canonical gospels are only a fraction of the gospels that were written. The rest were either neglected or suppressed for nearly a millennium before re-emerging by accidental discoveries. Scholars continue to debate whether material in the so-called Gnostic gospels (which promote a mystical, unearthly Jesus) is just as ancient as the material in the canonical Gospels.[14]

"Taken separately or together," conclude CK, "these considerations are surely sufficient to raise doubts about the reliability of the historical testimony on which Christian claims about Jesus are founded" (15). There are deeper problems than this, but I shall say more about those at the end of this chapter.

The Resurrection Claim

The claim that is most outrageous to the secular mind is that Jesus of Nazareth rose from death, appeared to his disciples, and then "ascended to heaven." This alleged event, more than anything else, is traditionally regarded as spectacular evidence that Jesus in fact had the divine authority that his followers claimed for him.

At this point, I cannot withhold injecting an obvious argument that CK do not use: while there is no way to directly disprove an alleged miraculous historical event that happened two millennia ago, why should anyone believe it today, given that, in retrospect, Christianity appears to be just another sect that can be explained by naturalistic sociology? After all, the imminent apocalypse that both Jesus and Paul made the cornerstone of their ministry never happened, and history continued to unfold since then as it always has. History is littered with Christian movements that humiliated themselves by taking that prophecy seriously, only to suffer a Great Disappointment. This is all the more reason to question the historicity of the supposed resurrection story that started the movement.

CK cite the following problems:

(1) Christians cannot consistently believe this miracle while invoking methodological naturalism to debunk the claims of other faith traditions that also claim miracles by their founders.
(2) The resurrected Jesus, say CK, was apparently witnessed only by his followers, raising the question of whether it met the criterion of "public evidence." Then CK make what I

consider to be a major logical mistake by adding a parenthetical statement to the effect that Paul was an apparent exception by having "his vision of the risen Jesus."[15] Obviously, having a vision of an event is not the same as being a witness of the event itself. But to CK's credit, at least they put it in parentheses.

(3) Resurrecting a person who has been dead three days is medically incredible because of the tremendous deterioration that happens over that time.

(4) A body ascending into heaven is more problematic now that heaven can't be conceived as being located just above the "solid dome" of the sky.

(5) Finally, there is the problem of why a benevolent deity would raise from the dead a single favored individual while leaving so many innocents in their graves. Is there any way to defend a claim so outrageous? If not, what hope is there of winning a favorable hearing for the rest of what Christianity has to say about Jesus?

Agnosticism and Christian Minimalism

Having laid out five major objections, CK set out to argue that belief is still preferable to agnosticism. That is, they assert that it "makes sense even for *non-Christians* to regard belief in at least some Christian claims—those that Christianity shares with other theistic religions—as rationally preferable to their rejection; that it is intellectually better, consequently, to affirm those claims than to deny them; better also than to refuse to affirm them" (17).

Further, CK argue that it "makes sense for those who find themselves engaging ultimate reality in and through their participation in the Christian tradition to have a similar attitude (that it is 'better') toward certain claims that are particular to that tradition and are not shared by others" (17). But they hasten to add that "better" means that the argument for belief is only somewhat stronger than not affirming said beliefs, and that the judgment of "better" is tentative, pending new information that may tip the balance in another direction. This tentative stance is what they call a kind of "Christian minimalism" (18).

There are two senses in which one can be minimalist: first, one may believe fewer things than many others in one's tradition, and second, one may affirm that one's beliefs are only minimally more likely to be true than false.

CK say their brand of minimalism will employ both of those strategies, but hope to show that it is not necessary to be a "maximally minimalist," a minimalist to the extreme—to the extent that some popular authors (Gerd Ludemann and John Shelby Spong are singled out) in the so-called historical Jesus debate have claimed. CK argue that such scholars are not really minimalists so much as they are actually "liberals," in the sense that they over-estimate the strength of their reasons for supposing that they know what actually happened, and therefore feel entitled to "correct" tradition accordingly.[16]

By contrast, CK note that the kind of minimalist they are referring to holds Christian beliefs that are "significantly constrained by philosophical objections and contemporary scientific consensus (which distinguishes her from more conservative evangelical or neo-orthodox believers) but also holds beliefs that, despite those constraints, she has reason to think do justice to the received testimony of the Christian tradition (which sets her apart from liberal believers in the sense just defined)" (18).

CK defend their minimalism against the charge that minimalism will be "blown about by every wind of doctrine" and that it amounts to a Christian agnosticism. The obvious solution to the problem of doctrinal instability, say CK, is "fideism," which is a total close-mindedness to all potentially contrary evidence, on the supposition that one already has the truth and therefore has nothing left to learn. But even if one accepts that epistemologically arrogant option, it is made problematic by the dilemma of knowing the proper moment to become totally close-minded.

The Christian agnostic, argue CK, is actually just as dogmatic as the fideist in that agnostics also close their minds to any new evidence, but for a different reason: because truth is unknowable it is merely useless speculation. Both alternatives, therefore, for different reasons close themselves off from any new learning and openness to new discoveries.

What separates CK's minimalism from Christian agnostics[17] is, first, CK's unwillingness to decide in advance that no progress in assessing Christian claims can be made, and second, their conviction that pursuing the question of what is really the case, what is really true, is not just an intellectual game but also an urgent religious responsibility. That quest is for them "the gospel."

This does not mean that agnosticism is always wrong. There may indeed be questions that one has good reasons for thinking may never be answered. Yet, CK argue, the purpose of their book is to show that the most important questions raised by the claims of Christianity are not among those.

But if it turns out that the basic claims of Christianity (e.g., that there is a benevolent God in charge of the universe) are untrue, CK admit that it would make no sense to act in accordance with a set of claims one really sees no way at all of evaluating or confirming.[18] Such would constitute a Christian (fideist) policy that CK think would be inconsistent with the most fundamental tenet of Christianity, which is that "this ultimate reality... has disclosed something of itself, such that humans can respond to it" (20).[19]

CK reject Josh McDowell's "black and-white decision procedures" of "evidence that demands a verdict," Plantinga's assertion that core Christian beliefs are "properly basic" and thus justified until they encounter a specific "defeater,"[20] as well as the agnostic's dictum that "it is always wrong to form beliefs unless a case can be made that would convince a neutral observer."[21]

Instead, they carve out a standard for belief that is different than Plantinga's approach (which demands that skeptics prove a negative), and they accept a belief as justified when it is merely "more likely than not."[22] In this minimalism, it is permissible to believe even in cases where the "objective" evidence is very close to neutral, and one is permitted to have a strength of practical commitment that may and often does exceed the certainty of one's belief. The ethical/logical basis for this view is that it keeps alive the search for truth, which CK feel is an ethical obligation, although the search may destabilize belief. This approach also is not as biased against disconfirmation (immunizing) as Plantinga, who privileges Christian tradition and whose position would always place the burden of proof on the skeptic.[23]

Against the charge that they contradict themselves by allowing faith commitment to outrun the certainty of belief, CK reply that they are not defending commitment in the absence of reasons to believe. Then they make a conditional statement: "But if we do have reason to believe—reason to believe, that is, that a claim of world-shattering, life-defining importance is more likely than not to be actually true—then we have reason not only to hope that this claim is actually true but to guide our thoughts and actions by that claim and its implications" (21). It remains to be seen if they can produce that reason in subsequent chapters.[24]

CK admit that they cannot make a one-size-fits-all case for Christian minimalism. Some of their conclusions, they think, will have a claim on the attention of all rational agents who are concerned about ultimacy. Other conclusions will be fully credible only to those whose thinking has been shaped by Christian tradition. Their ambition is to present at least some intra-Christian claims in a way that outsiders can at least say, *"Had I had the experiences in question,* I would be justified in holding these beliefs" (21).

Some other important Christian claims, they admit, will fail to meet even this lower standard (articulated above). They argue that Christians may still responsibly hold such beliefs, so long as they honestly acknowledge not only the evidence for the claim in question but also the reasons for doubting it.

CK admit they are not offering "knock down" arguments against or for Christian orthodoxy. Their ambition is not to convert "all rational agents" to, or from, belief in "the most robust of Christian claims about the nature and significance of what occurred in the events surrounding the life of a certain ancient rabbi" (22).

Instead, they claim to defend "a way of understanding the natural world as stemming from a not-less-than-personal ultimate reality, a way of conceiving divine action that is compatible with scientific methods and results, and a way of interpreting the New Testament resurrection claims that we think remains plausible for men and women in the twenty-first century" (22). They pursue this goal "in full awareness of the depth of the predicament of belief in an era that is unusually…subject to reasons for doubt" (22).

Some Final Summary Notes

I must first express appreciation for CK taking on this challenging and sensitive subject. Those who were raised "in the faith" but who grow up unable to support the traditional faith of their parents, have for too long been treated like disrespectful, rebellious children who need a good spanking and should be ashamed of themselves. But in light of the way each era changes the ground of belief, the more appropriate metaphor would be a child being punished for outgrowing the clothes their parents bought them.

Second, as I have already mentioned in my footnotes, I think that CK were handicapped in their discussion of this subject by not having in their conceptual vocabulary the distinction between "public" versus "private" evidence, just as Clifford was in his 1877 essay. It is private evidence that distinguishes the person who has been raised in the Christian tradition from a person of equal intelligence and learning who has been raised in a secular environment. It is the difference in private evidence that separates a person who has had a "mystical" experience from those who haven't.

Third, I am puzzled by the fact that CK do not discuss a basis for truth or logic other than coherence (such as mathematics) or correspondence theory (science) in the first chapter. The theory of pragmatism as a justification for belief is analogous to consequentialist ethics as an alternative to traditional command ethics in which there is a God who commands you to follow certain rules. Even when you do not accept God as an authority, you can still develop an ethic based on "good" and "bad" consequences of certain kinds of behavior. The truth of Jehovah, for example, was presumably established consequentially by the fact that when the people rallied around a military leader invoking Jehovah's authority, they won battles. When rebellion and anarchy reigned within the tribe, they lost battles and blamed it on disloyalty to Jehovah. The truths about the concepts of heaven and hell in the afterlife were most probably discovered consequentially as ingenious ways to control people's behavior in this life.

Fourth, as mentioned earlier, I believe CK missed another fundamental reason for doubting Christian theology. Put simply, it is that the naturalistic historical trajectory of Christianity implies a naturalistic beginning. This is similar to doubt #4, which was "the [scandalous] state of the historical evidence" (11). But that only referred to the embarrassing state of the founding documents of Christianity, the so-called "gospels." That problem was potentially surmountable, had the subsequent history of Christianity gloriously surmounted those difficulties by producing a religious movement that was fundamentally superior to all others that went before it. But the unfolding history of Christianity with its perennial internecine warfare, embarrassing scandals, inquisition and pogroms, conquest and domination over "inferior" cultures in the name of Jesus, and with its continuous doctrinal fragmentation over differing interpretation of scriptures, gives the objective observer no compelling reason to hypothesize, after the fact, that Christianity alone was founded upon a supernatural miracle of any kind, including the incarnation or the resurrection. That apologists still make the attempt at all is presumably only because of their nonnegotiable presuppositions.

Fifth, the developments in the field of historical Jesus studies in 2012 may warrant a comment beyond my previous footnotes. Bart Ehrman's publication of *Did Jesus Exist? The Historical Argument for Jesus of Nazareth*,[25] the devastating rebuttals by Richard Carrier,[26] and Earl Doherty's 34-part point-by-point response,[27] may indicate a tipping point in secular scholarship against the very existence of a historical Jesus. It seems arguable whether a purely mythical Jesus is more devastating to Christian theology than Ehrman's (and Schweitzer's) conclusion that Jesus was in fact a psychotic, failed apocalypticist. At least the mythical Jesus subscriber can argue that such unflattering characterizations of a historical Jesus are false on purely historical-critical grounds.

Finally, I am grateful to CK for showing that doing Christian theology does not consist merely of constructing "immunizing" arguments for sectarian doctrines.

---

[1] Richard Rice, *Reason and the Contours of Faith* (Riverside, Calif.: La Sierra University Press, 1991), 50.
[2] William James, "The Will to Believe," http://educ.jmu.edu//~omearawm/ph101willtobelieve.html. Originally a lecture to the Philosophical Clubs of Yale and Brown Universities, published in *New World*, June 1896.
[3] I retrieved this from my journal for 7/31/2010.
[4] CK grant some exceptions. Among those exceptional authors and books, they list Brian McLaren's *A New Kind of Christianity: Ten Questions that are Transforming the Faith* (New York: HarperOne 2010) and his *Everything Must Change: Jesus, Global Crisis, and a Revolution of Hope* (Nashville: Thomas Nelson, 2007).
[5] The authors use "ultimate" where we would normally use "ontological," which means the way things really are, as opposed to the way things may only appear to fallible humans.
[6] This of course alludes to the life and death of the earthly or historical Jesus.
[7] CK list John Shelby Spong as one of many who advocate this strategy, citing his *Why Christianity Must Change or Die: A Bishop Speaks to Believers in Exile* (San Francisco: HarperCollins, 1999).
[8] This appears to be A. Schweitzer's stance.
[9] CK also express some skepticism regarding this particular achievement in Chapter 3.
[10] Since Paul de Vries, a philosopher at Wheaton College, coined the term "methodological naturalism" in 1986, it has gained popularity. I prefer it because it incorporates the word "methodological," which explicitly differentiates it from a metaphysical or ontological assumption.
[11] Here is where the concept of "private evidence" should be used to explain the shift in the way people interpret events.
[12] Bart Ehrman cites the problem of evil as the reason why he gave up his

Christian faith. See *Jesus Interrupted: Revealing the Hidden Contradictions in the Bible (and Why We Don't Know About Them)* (New York: HarperOne, 2009), 273.

[13] I can't count the times apologists have told me, "Oh, but that is to be expected, because witnesses to an event always contradict each other! That is why we know that this is real history, and not some conspiracy!" They seem not to notice that they are effectively admitting that the gospels are no different than any other human report, and that none of these accounts are from actual witnesses.

[14] In his book *Lost Christianities: The Battles for Scripture and Faith We Never Knew* (New York: Oxford University Press, 2003), Bart Ehrman analyzes the work of the heresiologists and the historians of early Christianity to discover who the various contending Christian factions were and why all lost to the eventual winners, who declared themselves orthodox and got to decide what books made it into the canon.

[15] Since when does having a vision of a resurrected dead person constitute being a witness to that person's physical resurrection? If I have a vision of my deceased mother, then am I a witness to her resurrection? CK appear to be alluding to I Cor. 15:5-8. There, Paul is equating his own visionary experience with that of Cephas, the twelve, the 500, James, and all the apostles. But if this equation is valid, and we know from Gal. 1:16 that Paul's encounter was visionary, then this logically means all the appearances were visionary, just like his.

[16] The distinction CK make between minimalists and liberals seems to be that liberals overestimate the strength of their evidence, whereas minimalists do not, a distinction that seems quite subjective and self-serving. I have been seriously following the scholarly historical Jesus debate for about eight years and think it is a far more serious problem for traditional Christianity than mainstream Christian scholarship supposes.

[17] CK ignore the difference between hard (capital "A") Agnostics and soft (small "a") agnostics. The former believe it is impossible to know the truth; the latter only deny present knowledge, but do not deny in principle the possibility of acquiring knowledge in the future.

[18] Here and elsewhere, CK appear to have no awareness or respect for the logic of pragmatism, which is strictly consequentialist or functional in nature. I think it a mistake not to mention that line of reasoning, even if it is to dismiss it.

[19] CK's logic appears to be: if in fact nothing was disclosed, then no response is required. But pragmatism would allow the justification of a functional belief that was not necessarily "disclosed."

[20] That is, placing the burden of proof on the skeptic to prove a negative.

[21] This is similar to Clifford's ethic of belief, except that, unlike Clifford, it defines "sufficient" belief as one that would convince a neutral observer.

[22] This is still problematic, as a probability can be manipulated from virtual impossibility to near certainty, depending of the presuppositions built

into that calculation. An example is how cosmologists have changed the near impossibility of the "fine tuning" of a godless universe, which would be needed to make life possible on earth, to near certainty by merely presupposing an infinite multiverse.

[23] This usually forces the skeptic to prove a negative. It seems to me that this discussion is considerably impoverished without the concept of Rice's "private evidence" and William James's concept of a dead, or near-dead, hypothesis. After all, we do not have conscious control over what we believe, and "public evidence" is judged by our private evidence.

[24] This reminds one of Pascal's Wager, which I consider to be unsound because one has no direct conscious control over one's beliefs, and there are many competing beliefs to bet on besides the Christian one.

[25] Bart Ehrman, *Did Jesus Exist? The Historical Argument for Jesus of Nazareth* (New York: HarperOne, 2012).

[26] Richard Carrier, "Ehrman on Jesus: A Failure of Facts and Logic," http://freethoughtblogs.com/carrier/archives/1026/.

[27] Earl Doherty, "Response to Bart Ehrman's *Did Jesus Exist?*" http://vridar.org/other-authors/earl-dohertys-response-to-bart-ehrmans-did-jesus-exist/.

2

AN ARID FAITH WELL DEFENDED

A Reflection on Chapter 2, "The Ultimate Reality"

William Breer

In this book in general and this chapter in particular Clayton and Knapp (hereafter CK) seem to be trying to guide intellectual non-theologians onto a path that will allow them to develop or hold onto a faith with varying degrees of connection to traditional, orthodox Christianity. The first chapter concisely presents the difficulties contemporary intellectuals are likely to have with Christian views about the nature of God and Christ.

At the end of Chapter 1, the authors begin to define their reasons to believe that there is an ultimate reality lying behind the reality we as post-enlightenment Westerners perceive with our common sense. They argue that their concept of ultimate reality lies behind the reality studied and interpreted by modern science with its methodological naturalism. Common-sense perceptions of reality and the specific, measurable reality that reveals itself in methodological naturalism have a complex relationship. Many cultural and religious groups have fervent beliefs in supernatural realities that lie behind the ordinary reality apprehended by our senses. But for intellectuals in this culture there is usually a striving to fuse common-sense reality with the reality uncovered by scientific research. This drive is to make the reality verified by methodological naturalism the only reality to which a sane person can adhere.

Chapter 2 is densely and concisely written. In general, concepts are clearly defined. CK open this chapter by briefly referencing their core hypothesis of the first chapter to lay a foundation for this one:

> In the opening chapter, we stated that hypothesis as "the belief or wager that behind or beyond all things, at the beginning of everything we see and know, there exists an ultimate reality that in some sense intended us (or things like us) to be here and—again in some sense—desires our flourishing." Because it is capable of something like intention and something like desire, this ultimate reality...must be conceived, on this hypothesis, as having properties at least similar to those of a person. (23)

After this foundational beginning, the authors go on to describe their position as Christian minimalism. For them Christian minimalism means both a willingness to embrace only the most basic and logically sustainable elements of doctrine and a minimal commitment to cling to such elements in the face of contrary evidence. They describe themselves as seeking the most plausible version of Christian theism that is still consistent with what they believe to be the tradition's core commitments. The authors here neglect to define and explore what they mean by "plausible." This is a rare omission in a work that usually lays foundations methodically and defines terms appropriately.

In this and related sections of the book CK describe their target audience. It is those who are uncertain that any form of distinctly Christian belief in God is still plausible in an age of science and religious pluralism. They are not writing to strengthen the faith of—or marshal arguments for—those already committed to Christianity or any other faith devoted to a transcendent God.

Science and Its Limitations

CK are concerned that resistance to their ideas may arise because these ideas are regarded as metaphysical speculation rather than "science." They point to the extraordinary value our culture places on inquiry following scientific rules of inquiry. By contrast, in pre-scientific times and other cultures conclusions are often derived from speculation. In CK's words: "Metaphysical reflections are indeed suspect, in our view, when they compete head-to-head with scientific explanations of matters that lend themselves to scientific investigation... Still, it's a mistake to think that science therefore becomes the authority for all questions" (25).

The authors cite some issues in the general realm of science that are problematic for methodological naturalism. For example: what preceded the Big Bang? CK say that it is widely agreed that anything that may lie in the realm of the supernatural is beyond the scope of such investigation. However, this is hard to distinguish from a "God of the gaps" argument. For the faithful this line of reasoning poses the dilemma that new scientific theories can always close the gaps. Atheist groups generally claim, often prematurely, the elimination of gaps.

CK also turn their attention to quantum physics. It confronts us with philosophical questions that physics itself may never be able to answer, such as the indeterminacy of quantum reality, the role of observers, and subjectivity in measurement—the problem of the "collapse of the wave function" (25). In the current state of quantum physics, philosophical questions are largely confined to the behavior of very small particles, but quantum phenomena seem to be creeping up the size scale. This area may pose increasing problems for methodological naturalism.

A related issue is science's—really, scientism's—growing claim to be all we need to explore reality. This effort ignores epistemology and has science claiming things it cannot own. CK take a philosophical look at the issue and argue that the ability to reach empirically justified results depends on the underlying assumptions about the nature of the reality being studied. If these assumptions are not accurate, the results will not be valid. In many cases science cannot justify the most fundamental assumptions it makes, such as the assumption that natural laws are unchanging.

As concrete examples of this thinking, CK note Dawkins' proclamation that the empirical parts of biology suffice to demonstrate that all talk of God is a delusion. This proclamation, of course, grossly overstates the evidence. CK add an even more extreme declaration from philosopher Daniel Dennett to the effect that Darwinism is a universal acid that will dissolve everything in its path (26).

Logical positivism, another philosophy proclaiming the dominance of scientific methodology over other ways of knowing, takes the matter a step further, asserting that, according to CK, "only 'observation statements,' and statements directly inferred from them, have genuine meaning; all other statements are, strictly speaking, meaningless" (27).

The philosophical problem with this extreme logical positivist approach, according to CK, is that this principle did not satisfy its own criteria for meaning: it was itself not based on, or derived from, any observation statement. This points out a need to carefully examine science from a framework of philosophy and epistemology in order to be sure we are not trying to scientifically measure things beyond the scope of science.

Ultimate Reality as Mind and Agent

Next CK sketch what they contend is the mind-like quality of ultimate reality. Here they seek to move beyond the notion of God as an impersonal force to a God with some qualities of personhood. The authors note that they will proceed very cautiously in their discussion of this quality of ultimate reality. They stress that all assertions about this reality are provisional and somewhat tenuous—in perfect accord with their Christian minimalism.

CK begin their argument by noting that the universe appears to be designed for life, and from here the argument gets complex. The well-known anthropic principle is the center of the argument. One conclusion of this line of reasoning is that our universe is finely tuned, at least in its initial conditions prior to the Big Bang, so that processes could lead to the emergence of intelligent life. This leads to the statement: "If so, whatever the UR [ultimate reality] is, it must be capable of purposive action" (31).

CK are eager to separate this idea from intelligent design, as it is encountered in science/religion debates. Intelligent design as discussed by Meyer in Signature in the Cell seems to claim status as a scientific theory.[1] However, as CK indicate, intelligent design advocates are not really offering a scientific theory, but rather a philosophical argument that has a different nature and different standards for exploration and proof than would a theory that really meets the criteria to justify the label science (34). CK are arguing for another kind of intelligent design. This is design by a purposive ultimate reality. This kind of idea can expect intense opposition from those who oppose any idea of theistically influenced creation in the public square.

CK spend some time on the idea that there are many universes. The multiverse idea is where some scientists have gone to explain some serious statistical problems. Statistical studies suggest that it is almost impossible that the universe emerged as it is by mere chance or that life emerged by natural selection acting on random variation.

One way to deal with these statistical problems while avoiding any kind of theism would be to hypothesize an infinite number of universes. With an infinite number of universes, anything is statistically possible. By this means we can find theoretical justification for the idea that life in our highly improbable universe emerged by chance with no need to consider design. It just emerged because with so many statistical opportunities, it was bound to happen somewhere and we are in that somewhere.

The authors spend some time refuting the idea that the multiverse theory explains our universe without the need for intent, design, or agency. The objections are: the theory is really not science since it could never be empirically tested, it only moves the problem to a higher level, and it is still necessary to explain why initial conditions created even one universe capable of developing intelligent life. If each universe has its own laws of physics, can anything scientific or authoritative be said about the resulting theoretical chaos? If these multiple universes all follow the same laws, that implies mind-like properties to the laws since they move as non-physical forces from universe to universe (33).

CK make some powerful arguments against the multiverse theory, and I am convinced by their argument that this theory is untestable and therefore unscientific. What this dispute comes down to is two competing theories, each of which is beyond the kind of proof scientists seek and require for belief. So one reviews the arguments and selects one; it comes down to preference. I suspect the reasons for our preferences are deeply rooted in our individual psyches.

The authors also believe that the mind-like or person-like quality of the ultimate reality neither requires nor excludes that this reality has other qualities. There are several reasons for stressing this property. It means that the ultimate reality is also an agent capable of forming the universe with something like intentions. This is essential if they want to argue for the creation of the universe in anything like Christian terms. After careful argument, CK conclude that this is the most adequate conception of the ultimate reality (37).

Is the Mind/Agent Good and Does It Care About Us?

What is the nature of ultimate reality's relationship with humankind? Does it care about us? Is it good as we humans understand goodness? CK begin the argument for the goodness of the mind/agent with this question: "[W]hat conclusions about the moral nature of the UR follow from the assumption that the UR has intentionally brought about the existence of a universe in which it was possible for rational and moral agents—that is, for persons—to evolve" (38)? One issue inherent in this question is whether this ultimate reality created us for its own sake. Did it need us or was its existence enriched by our creation? After careful argument CK conclude that this reality, as they have described it, could not have needed us (39).

With the conclusion that the creator did not need us, it follows that it must have created us for our sake. We were created as sheer generosity, sheer love for finite others. The authors go on to argue that the mind/agent provides us with moral guidance. Indeed, this becomes another argument for the caring nature of ultimate reality. They cite the work of Peter Berger, a sociologist, who finds evidence that human experience points in the direction of a benevolent reality that interacts with us to form conscience (40). In a broader sense the argument here is that the creator interacts with us in a moral way that leads to values and conscience.

CK conclude this chapter sensing that they have presented a good case for an ultimate reality that has much in common with the deity of the Abrahamic traditions. This deity is an infinite agent, not less than personal, and has performed at least one self-limiting act of creation motivated by agape. They also note that this ultimate reality has a "Christological tinge" in that it is compassionate and self-giving. The authors note, however, that one cannot derive the God of the Abrahamic tradition from the arguments in this chapter. They have not yet arrived at Allah or Yahweh.

A Faith of the Mind

CK have done well what they set out to do. They have tested Christian teachings by the scientific method and decided what remains believable. They have avoided metaphysical speculation and are not trying to justify the faith of those who are already deeply committed. What is the value of this? I think it does a service for a certain kind of intellectual who is interested in Christianity either academically or as a personal faith. These words are carefully chosen with "certain kind of intellectual" and "interested in Christianity" as key concepts. The certain kind of intellectual to whom I refer is one drawn to the endless debates about science and religion. In the context of America as a whole, this is a small and specialized audience. Those who are drawn here come in part because they are participants in a culture whose intellectuals value the results of scientific investigations as the highest, and in many cases the only, truth.

The prestige of science is so pervasive that it creates a situation in which some individuals feel they can only embrace a Christian faith if they can synthesize their faith in such a way that it has no conflict with science. Creationists attempt this by trying to pour science into a mold supposedly delineated by their faith. They look for science-like proofs of the Flood, etc. After much work they claim that they have found harmony and can now believe without ambivalence. Outsiders often find creationists' proofs less than convincing, so this approach only works for a small group.

At the other extreme are the neo-atheists who use the contemporary scientific worldview to deprive Christians of their faith. Certain atheists expend great energy demonstrating that events in the Bible are scientifically impossible and that the Bible is not a scientific monograph. Neo-atheist positions can be very troubling to those whose desires and instincts tell them to remain Christian, but who have been socialized to accept the ontological naturalism that is implicit in our culture. This cognitive dissonance fuels a lot of the effort that goes into the science/faith debate.

CK's current work targets these issues. They are building a case that it is possible to be an intellectual adhering to the dominant scientific epistemology of our culture and still cling to some (or a few) of the historical tenets of Christianity. The propositions that the authors feel withstand scientific scrutiny or at least have some hope of surviving this scrutiny are that ultimate reality is: (1) a personality, (2) the creator of us and the time/space in which we live and any other reality that might exist, (3) concerned with our well-being and moral behavior, and (4) characterized by compassion that is Christ-like and might be personified as Jesus.

The authors describe their arguments as tenuous and tentative. They are likely of interest to the target audience that includes sympathetic doubters and literate believers. However, these ideas are not likely to tap into the subsurface streams that structure faith and practice, and here I cannot help but to draw on my experience as a psychotherapist. CK write for the frontal cortex of the brain, the center that makes careful calculations about reality and then makes decisions based more or less on reason. Much more powerful is the limbic system where our emotions reside. I think that much of religious experience involves the limbic system, and if we can trust some recent research, a "religious center" resides in the temporal lobes.

There is substantial research suggesting that human beings arrive at their conclusions and behavior as a result of a mixture of frontal cortex activity and limbic input. It is likely that the limbic input is the more important. This is offered not because CK should have factored in the limbic system, but to offer a suggestion on why many may find this work mildly interesting but unsatisfying. It is too religious for those who have an emotionally driven agnosticism or atheism and not religious enough for those who have an emotionally-driven need to believe.

A more cognitive objection is that the authors' conclusions are often a result of a long, logical "decision tree" where a series of propositions are reviewed and a conclusion selected from alternatives. Each step is necessary to move on to the next. At times it is likely that there may be more than one way to decide at a particular juncture. Not accepting the authors' decision at each step would lead to a different result. Hence the results are plausible, but sometimes only weakly convincing.

CK's construct for an intellectual faith is interesting and many Christians will probably find it somewhat faith-supporting. CK have argued well and their case meets something like a law court's preponderance-of-evidence standard.

A Faith for the Heart

Most of our contemporary Western intellectual culture is massively dominated by scientific thinking. If science cannot see it and study it, it does not exist. The propositions of most religions cannot be seen and studied, so the religious intellectual has a dilemma: disregard the dominant way of knowing prescribed by our culture, or enter a realm where other rules decide what is real, a world of private evidence.

CK's work will appeal to many religious intellectuals. They may turn there hoping to find a way to preserve their faith in both science and a revealed religion, and I've already touched upon some of the difficulties. But the question remains: do CK offer the only resolution to educated participants in Western culture struggling with the science/faith conflict?

There are other answers. They tend to fall into the forbidden terrain of metaphysical speculation, and they are various and complex. Discussion of them is well beyond the scope of this brief essay, but I will at least list some alternatives for the faithful. Science in its more humble manifestations does not claim to be the exclusive arbiter of what is real and what is not. There are realms of metaphysics beyond the reach of science. Philosophers and theologians can argue whether the reality perceived here is as real as that described by science.

Within science itself, quantum mechanics suggests the need for some modesty about what we can know. If there is ever a comprehensive integration of science and religion, it will probably begin with quantum mechanics. Nonlocal space, reality determined by observation, and quantum entanglements that instantly span the cosmos certainly provide a place for speculation about what has been perceived as the supernatural.

Another approach to saving one's faith is to retreat into a rigid adherence to biblical inerrancy and fundamentalist literalism. This simply asserts either that science just does not get it right, or that religion is another kind of reality and examining it scientifically is a form of reductionism. This runs the risk of creating a brittle cognitive structure for faith that is all too easily assaulted in the modern world. There are other ways to use Scripture that revere it without putting faith into such direct conflict with common-sense reality.

William James' stress on the centrality of experience in faith is of importance here. Our direct personal experience with God and/or the supernatural is what matters. Various faith traditions offer ways of experiencing the divine that are convincing to those who pursue this path. There are mystical traditions in the major and minor religions that use a path of prayer and meditation to attain a direct experience of God. Embracing a mystical tradition opens the door to innumerable, conflicting cosmologies and paths that can discredit the whole concept, at least in the eyes of certain outside observers. Some problems must be accepted as an unavoidable side effect of giving central role to experience in the realm of faith.

The near-worship of science in our society is a culturally derived value. Another culturally derived value is the stress on building the individual into a fortress of power and knowledge. Ambiguity, unknowability, and mystery are not compatible with fortress-like individuality. This ideology pursues absolute knowledge of reality, with science as one's roadmap to such knowledge. If one wishes to preserve a faith in the God of Christianity, it helps to question all of these culturally derived assumptions.

Science almost daily adds complexity to its portrait of the cosmos and our biosphere, and the most brilliant specialists only grasp a narrow segment of this interwoven complexity. Is there any reason to believe that the human mind is really adequate to grasp ultimate reality? It is becoming increasingly clear that Homo sapiens may not have been endowed with the IQ to grasp the complexities in which we live. So one route to spiritual peace is to accept mystery, rely on experience, and enjoy the peace that faith can bring.

[1] Stephen C. Meyer, *Signature in the Cell: DNA and the Evidence for Intelligent Design* (New York: HarperOne, 2009).

3

FROM THEODICY TO ANTHROPODICY

A Reflection on Chapter 3, "Divine Action and the Argument from Neglect"
Lee F. Greer

Philip Clayton and Steven Knapp (hereafter CK) are theologians who welcome the advances of modern science, while critical of the fundamentalist rejection of science. Clayton is an advocate of the "non-interventionist, objective, divine action" (NIODA) program. CK propose a well-considered theodicy that is measurably superior to most theodicies in its seriousness and candor. I critically reflect on their program, noting that our agreement on ethical goals makes our dialogue a constructive engagement.

Theodicy-making and the Classical Problem of Suffering and Evil

"Theodicy" was coined by the moderate Enlightenment[1] multi-talented[2] Gottfried Leibniz in 1710[3] by combining two Greek words: θεός, god or deity, and δίκη, translated in recent centuries as "justice."[4] Leibniz's *Théodicée* was partly responding to the characterization of the problem as rationally insoluble in the *Dictionnaire Historique et Critique* (1697, 1702) by Huguenot and Radical Enlightenment scholar Pierre Bayle. Like John Milton in *Paradise Lost* (1667; Book I), Leibniz sought "to justify the ways of God to men." His solution appealed to the presumed goodness of God, a divine "pre-established harmony," human freedom, and the balance of good to evil in the world. In *Candide, ou L'Optimisme* (1759), Voltaire satirized Leibniz and his theodicy in the character Dr. Pangloss who stubbornly holds "that all is for the best in this best of all possible worlds."

Attempts to resolve the theistic problem of suffering and evil have a long history in Western classical, Jewish, Christian, and Islamic thought, as well as in other traditions. Today, in the Leibnizian tradition, a theodicy is an active defense of God's allowance of evil in light of the classical divine characteristics of omnipotence, omniscience, and omnibenevolence. Most modern theodicies propose solutions modifying the first two in order to save the third, omnibenevolence. CK's *apologia* is firmly in this category.

A trenchant statement of the problem of evil is the famous *Tetralemma* of Epicurus (341-270 BCE):

- α – *Is God willing to prevent evil, but not able? Then he is not omnipotent.*
- β – *Is he able but not willing? Then he is malevolent.*
- γ – *Is God both able and willing? Then how come evil?*
- δ – *Is he neither able nor willing? Then why call him God?*

Theodicy also entails (1) the divine revelation problem and (2) the Darwinian problem. (1) Why is there divinely endorsed evil in the "revealed" scriptures, whether the Hebrew Torah and prophets, the Christian New Testament, or the Quran? One cannot ignore the multilayered textual claims (important to conservatives in these traditions) for divine agency in authorizing, participating, and justifying of heinous evil, including wars of conquest and plunder, genocides, and other moral atrocities such as slavery and misogyny. All of these are approvingly or grudgingly attributed to God and his partisans.[5]

(2) The Darwinian problem:[6] Why do sentient beings suffer and go extinct so prodigiously throughout the long, wandering, emergent experimenting in the evolution of life and its diversity? Why is evolution so marked with numerous dead-end extinctions, including so many extinct human species and groups of the genus *Homo*? Why should the most creative, novelty-producing episodes of evolution depend so particularly on mass extinctions? Furthermore, why are the adapted reproductive processes so profligate, wasteful, and wantonly spendthrift of lives and potential lives? In the final soliloquy in Camus' *L'Étranger*,[7] the condemned Meursault tells the priest, that there is "only one class of men, the privileged class"—those who are alive. As living humans we have already won the Mendelian lottery and run the Malthusian gauntlet—just to be born, only to face the Darwinian sieve for the next generation. And once we arrive, the joys, the good fortune, as well as the sufferings and untimely deaths are distributed so unevenly.

That the Hebrew and Christian scriptures (both anthologies with long textual histories and oral prehistories) do not provide a coherent solution to the problem of suffering has been known for a long time. Bart Ehrman has convincingly so argued yet again.[8] The most penetrating parts of the Hebrew scriptures, however, do not lightly dismiss the problem. A few passages especially from *Ecclesiastes* and the poetic mid-section of *Job* starkly and poignantly enunciate the struggle to understand.

The Argument from Neglect

From the broad sweep available, CK choose a limited statement of the problem of evil to which they respond. They cite the statement of the problem by philosophical theologian, Wesley Wildman, who argues that the existence of suffering indicates a divine neglect, and that this makes the idea of a personal deity untenable because it does not "pass the test of parental moral responsibility."[9]

Wildman's objection is itself a narrowing of the problem, because it only considers divine neglect, bypassing scriptural evil by abandoning the traditional personhood of God. CK do not address the Darwinian or biblical problems, despite striving to retain a proximally orthodox theology more or less referable to Scripture.

CK do well to largely ignore the traditional "free will" theodicy, which so enthralls many conservative theists. "Free will" has never been an adequate solution. In human morality, no one ever argues that stopping a criminal from harming others is a violation of "free will" whatever the nature of volition or biological agency. So why should a personal God get away with such a justification of neglect of evil, i.e., bystander guilt?[10] Even limiting the problem to divine neglect leaves no small challenge for their divine-person *apologia*.

In defending person-language theism, CK set out to accomplish two tasks: (1) Postulate "that there may be a good reason why a personal and active God" (45) either cannot or chooses not to do what we as moral human beings would instinctively expect an omnibenevolent or any benevolent agent to do. (2) Avoid the *reductio ad absurdum* of constraining divine action to irrelevancy or pointlessness—omnipotence, omniscience *reductio*. They in part capitulate to Epicurus' *Tetralemma* by compromising omnipotence, and maybe omniscience. Have they also compromised omnibenevolence?

At the outset, CK set a minimal standard of argument. Rather than seeking compelling and persuasive reasons for divine neglect, they only seek a "*plausible* explanation for apparent divine neglect"

(46). They proceed to minimize even further by asserting that their response need only be plausible "in the eyes of the relevant community of inquiry;" that is, to those "not already closed to the possibility" of person-language theism. As long as it is merely plausible and consistent, it will count as defeating Wildman's objection, they assert. Their minimization of the problem reduces the appeal to those outside their "community of inquiry," a community that seems to consist of those who begin from the same assumptions.

Our review will examine whether the CK theodicy convincingly passes not only Wildman's "parental responsibility" test, but more importantly whether it answers to the compelling broader challenge of theodicy. For only then can their considered efforts be of relevance to a wider informed audience.

CK's Hypothesis for Defeating the Argument from Divine Neglect

Marshaling concepts from science, philosophy of science, philosophy of mind, and kenotic (self-emptying) christologies, CK seek to meet the challenge as they have posed it. Their hypothesis is that God's purposes include creating a universe capable of bringing about the evolution of "finite rational agents capable of entering into communion with God" (46). Their argument is rooted in the theodicy of Irenaeus (third century CE), that divine neglect is necessary for "soul-making" or creation of moral agents, a type of "moral choice" theodicy. Hence, the universe must have laws/causal regularities which God does not override, to avoid hindering rational agency in the creatures intended. Two questions they pose in this context are as follows (46). (1) How law-like do the laws of nature have to be? Why can't God keep the regularities of nature long enough to evolve rational and autonomous creatures, but occasionally suspend the laws to prevent innocent suffering? In short, is there a way to violate the laws of the universe after all, for the sake of theodicy? (2) If God cannot override nature's regularities, then how can God perform any intentional actions within the universe? To the point, in a causally-implicate universe, how can we ascribe active moral intention to God? Very central questions indeed.

(1) *CK's first response to divine neglect and the "parental responsibility" test* (47). God could not suspend the laws even occasionally because it would be hard to see how rational and moral agency could evolve in such a universe. The pursuit of systematic knowledge of the natural world would not be possible. Human rational agency can grow because we can grow in understanding of the universe through scientific observation of natural regularities, because those regularities do not alter arbitrarily, through either human or divine subjective fiat. This is CK's regularity argument. So why can't the divine agent intervene at least *occasionally* to prevent or relieve human suffering, such as the Indian Ocean tsunami (Christmas, 2004) which claimed about 250,000 lives and untold suffering, or the Nazi Holocaust, or the shooting of the babies in Newtown Connecticut, or the millions of deaths every year from climate change, environmental degradation, contributing to child hunger, disease, etc.? Why tolerate this appalling level of suffering? CK respond that such violations of natural law would deprive the created finite agents of perceiving themselves as separate from God (49). CK offer a *not-even-once* (NEO) principle for divine intervention, because if God were to intervene at all, God would "incur ... the responsibility to intervene in every case" to prevent innocent suffering. The postulated deity only incurs a personal responsibility to intervene by intervening. It follows then, that if he never intervened (not-even-once!) *he would*

never incur any responsibility at all. Next they reframe this "answer" by subdividing it into three answers:

- (a) *Forensic*—God could not explain or justify to others why he didn't intervene in other cases. This option CK feel is too anthropocentric. But isn't it already anthropocentric to conceptualize a personal deity with moral intentions to explain the world's unfairness?
- (b) *Unethical*—It would be unjust for God to intervene in only certain cases but not others, even with a "proportional intervention" to evil prevented or suffering alleviated. This response immediately concedes the central argument of fairness against theodicy itself. (i) Empirically the world is drastically unfair, even in an idyllic ecosystem or a happy family, let alone the world at large, from the poignantly happy to the desperately agonizing. (ii) Is the failure of a moral agent to intervene in all cases more moral than failure to intervene in some? This problem seems to be a byproduct of a personal-language theism.
- (c) *Metaphysical*—The universe would lose autonomy in a chain reaction if God disrupted natural law. It is not entirely clear whether this argument is primarily designed (i) to save natural law by arguing that causality would be lost by divine intervention, i.e., the "autonomy" of the universe, or more pointedly (ii) to save the "autonomy" of a personal God.

CK assert that "it is not obvious [to them at least] that the forensic, ethical, and metaphysical responses are fatally flawed; each one may offer some support for the 'not even once' principle" (50) So, they suggest that a combination of the ethical and metaphysical answers provide a more compelling response. On the contrary, every one of these flawed responses illustrates how the NEO principle rather than supporting instead undermines a theodicy project.

Then they also suggest that perhaps the universe has an *appearance* of regularity for all that science can observe, but that underneath that appearance God could be working miracles subtly and furtively to alleviate suffering (52). (a) Empirically the alleviation is ineffective because the suffering and unfairness are unalleviated. (b) Reducing the regularities of natural causality to an appearance is a surreptitious surrender of the NEO principle. (c) *Appearance* posits at least one *moral* contradiction—a divine deception, where a personal deity engages in the staging of false appearances of causal regularity. Data show that regularities in nature are not mere apparent phenomena, but ineradicably intrinsic in deep mathematically described causal patterns, from quantum mechanics to the biosciences, which are increasingly becoming quantitatively strong-inference, at least in the hands of the best practitioners.

CK acknowledge that apparent regularity still leaves open the argument that God helps some but not others, and is therefore ethically inconsistent—this concedes that the problem of unfairness is as unresolved as ever. They freely admit that the first set of responses are not convincing because (a) evolution of rational, autonomous creatures requires a universe with (we must add, *actual*) laws[11] and regularity, and (b) while divine intervention may be metaphysically possible, ignoring the contradiction, by having God intervene even subtly to help some but not others is immorally inconsistent, unfair, i.e., God would "*incur ... the responsibility to intervene in all cases*" (52; emphasis added). Why God would only *incur* responsibility when he starts helping, and not by nature of his moral agency as a person, is left entirely unclear. We don't excuse capable humans in the immediate presence of suffering or need. Whether acting or refraining, God would have inescapable moral responsibility as a person, as a moral agent. CK seem not to recognize this.

With such internal logical and ethical contradictions, CK's first response to Wildman's test of "parental responsibility" fails to meet their own standard for consistency and therefore plausibility, the broader problem of suffering and evil is as untouched and unresolved as ever. They propose a second response.

(2) *CK's second response* (52). Granting that God cannot intervene in ways that disturb the natural regularity of the universe, CK introduce a new claim to save moral divine intervention in some form. CK assert that there *must be* one "sphere of existence within the created universe where events are not determined by the natural regularities" of natural causality, i.e., the sphere of the "mental" or "the mind." Here they abandon the NEO principle, in the very place, the human brain, where NEO would be most needed to preserve freedom in an Irenaean world evolving moral agents. The question for theodicy is whether slipping in divine intervention actually helps solve the problem of divine neglect.

Violating the NEO Principle by Asserting "the Nonlawlike Nature of the Mental" (53)

The *ad hoc* rescue hypothesis is their appeal to the "emergent complexity" of the human brain. CK affirm that they are seeking a way to avoid dualism—the belief that humans have an "immaterial soul" which is a different substance with different rules from what constitutes the universe—energy and mass with attendant fields and states in space-time. Descrying substance dualism, while trying to avoid ontological monism, CK appeal to emergence, and then *de facto* treat the observed levels of emergent phenomena within the universe as separate causal substances (causal-persistent entities, ontologically self-contained with their own rules of causation, all for *gratis*), despite their claim to seek an emergent monist solution. In *Predicament*, their unspoken substance pluralism is comparable to the Leibnizian metaphysical pluralism. Contrary to all evidence, they seem to divorce the observed emergent phenomena from their particular causal embeddings in the universe. In so doing, CK ironically make the very mistaken category conflation that Leibniz himself warned against in his own explicit battle against ontological monism:

> "It is well to beware, moreover, lest in confusing substances with accidents, in depriving created substances [Leibniz' self-contradictory monadic pluralism] of action, one fall into Spinozism [ontological monism].... If the accidents [i.e., in our context, particular emergent phenomena] are not distinct form the substances; if it does not endure beyond a moment, and does not remain the same...any more than its accidents...: Why shall not one say, with Spinoza, that God is the only substance, and that creatures are only accidents or modifications?"[12]

Why not indeed? Precisely because of theology and theodicy, that conclusion (in modern terms, ontological monism) was the one that Leibniz then, and CK now, it seems must eschew at all costs.

Emergence is natural causality. Emergence is the "the arising of novel and coherent structures, patterns and properties during the process of self-organization in complex systems," although "emergence functions not so much as an explanation but rather as a descriptive term pointing to the patterns, structures or properties that are exhibited on the macro-scale."[13] Emergent properties are well established in the sciences, requiring no appeal to substance dualism or pluralism and are being given more rigorous understandings of the newer sciences of complexity with their non-linear mathematics of chaos and systems theories.[14] Emergence can be understood in terms of *synergy* which is "the combined (cooperative) effects that are produced by two or more particles, elements, parts or organisms – effects that are not otherwise attainable."[15] When there is a hierarchy of levels in a complex system, we have "synergies of scale." Properties occur at higher synergistic levels, which are not apparent at the more elemental component levels. Precisely modeling mathematically the emergent-chaotic behavior at higher synergistic levels may become utterly non-trivial, but not non-causal. Emergent phenomena are multitudinous in nature and involve the creative emergence or self-organization of novelty and intricate complexity in systems. Causation goes both up and down the synergistic levels of scale in an intricate web or "hairball" of causation, as being shown in preliminary but promising modeling of self-organizing evolving system behaviors. This includes the downward causation of biological agents acting in goal-oriented or "teleodynamic" fashion to alter their environments or relationships, including human semiotic (meaning-making) activity, all of which is consistent, as Terence Deacon points out, with physical causality but not in an eliminative, reductionist way.[16] *None of this data even weakly implies that these phenomena are causally-rooted outside of Nature* (substance dualism or pluralism), but on the contrary all of it strongly infers consistency with the inherent unity of the world.

CK then argue that in the higher levels of a complex system, such as "a person or society, the agents being studied have become so strongly individualized that it becomes questionable whether their actions can still be explained in terms of underlying laws." By assuming this they advocate a philosophical "anomalous monism"[17] or "not law-governed" monistic account of mind to *imply* that "mental events are not" governed by natural causation. In actuality, they go further and assert pluralistic ontological independence of agents (i.e., Leibnizian monadism). Whether citing a *faux* monism or appealing to pluralism or panentheistic dualism, CK's attempt to divorce emergent levels from their causal embeddings is precisely where CK go beyond any warrant from science. Emergent levels are not separate ontological substances, but causally inseparable and enmeshed.

To accept *Predicament*'s suggested "'anomalous' account of mind one must maintain that, despite the dependence of the mental on the physical, human actions are not determined by the operation of natural laws or regularities" (55; see Appended Note). By assertion against all evidence, CK simply brush away the argument that *the complete dependence is indeed emergent, both causally* dependent and computationally non-trivial. CK concede that "patterns of human action may be law*like*, and rigorous forms of quantitative social science may well be possible" (55; emphasis theirs). Indeed, as attested in numerous peer-reviewed published papers, rigorous and quantitative scholarship in the social sciences, sociobiology, evolutionary psychology, and ethology is increasingly possible. CK simply assert that "[these patterns] will not be equivalent to, and hence (in principle) reducible to, natural scientific laws" (55).[18] That assertion is contrary to all of the evidence, in part because all of the upward and downward causation reveals the causal embedding of the emergent levels within each other.

Systems-emergent phenomena such as self-organizing complexity, biological agency (including human agency), and social interaction do not require such a divorce from natural causality, anymore than software-generated imagery, content, interacting networks such as the internet, and the emergent self-optimization of evolutionary algorithms (also known as artificial intelligence or machine learning) are separable from the physical electronics and semiconductor physics of the hardware. In neither case is there evidence for such separation or any need for substance pluralism/dualism, but a systems-emergence in a unitary world, where freedom is possible (Appended Note).

CK note that Davidson's (now dated) "anomalous monism" proposition is physicalist, while asking, "But does monism *have* to be physicalist?" (55). They acknowledge further that models "in ecology or psychology are not unleashed from nature; they must remain consistent with physical laws" (55). Why must they remain so? *For the very obvious reason that these phenomena are according to all available evidence causally inseparable from and embedded in the physical world.* Asserting that "the leash turns out to be rather longer than one might have thought," CK claim that "what we need is a version of anomalous monism that moves beyond the physicalist assumptions" (55) of Donaldson.

Why do we need this? Why this special pleading? A "beyond the physical" is certainly not what the scientific disciplines in question need in order to advance rapidly, as they indeed already are. However, a "beyond the physical" is *precisely what CK need for their theodicy. That is, CK apparently need something akin to substance pluralism, idealism, or dualism for their theodicy*, just like Leibniz did. Leibniz invented monadic substance pluralism for his theodicy in order to combat the naturalistic threat of Spinozistic substance monism during the early Enlightenment. As the brilliant Leibniz clearly saw and defensively conceded in response to one inquiry (1714), "On the contrary, it is precisely by means of the Monads [his infinite number of interacting eternal 'substances'] that Spinozism is destroyed.... For there are as many true substances...as there are monads; *whereas according to Spinoza, there is but one sole substance. He would be right if there were no Monads*" (emphasis added).[19]

Like Leibniz before, CK seem conflicted, both tempted and repelled, but nevertheless haunted by ontological monism. Johann Gottfried

Herder observed: "What Leibniz was in his heart I may not know; but his *Theodicy*[,] just as many of his letters[,] show that, precisely in order not to be a Spinozist, he thought through his system."[20] In the German *Aufklärung* of the second half of the eighteenth century, the major figure Gotthold Lessing expressed his "fear" that Leibniz was a cryptic "Spinozist at heart." Even moderate Enlightenment luminary, David Hume, more radical in modernist admiration than in actuality, professed horror at that "hideous hypothesis, the doctrine of the simplicity of the universe, and the unity of that substance, in which [Spinoza] supposes both thought and matter to inhere."[21] The extent to which the prominent figures of the moderate Enlightenment from Leibniz to Locke, Voltaire, and Kant, shrank from, flirted with, and obsessed over ontological monism (Spinozism) can be seen in their frightened reaction to the subversive theological, philosophical, social, and democratic implications of the Radical Enlightenment—a clandestine movement from the seventeenth century radicals around Spinoza, Bayle, van Leenhoff, and van Dale through English radicals such as Anthony Collins and John Toland, to the French materialists like Meslier to Diderot, D'Holbach, D'Alembert, and Condorcet in the late eighteenth century. This unprecedented upheaval in Western thought and culture[22] still frames the intellectual culture wars today: Spinoza versus Leibniz.[23] The century and a half long struggle over ontological monism and its alternatives shaped the great German idealist Hegel's concept of dialectic. And through the German idealist Frederich Schelling this upheaval still influences the theology and theodicy of CK and kindred theologians today.[24]

Why did Leibniz take these metaphysical evasive measures? Of his own private notes and papers, Bertrand Russell commented: "Here, as elsewhere, Leibniz fell into Spinozism whenever he allowed himself to be logical; in his published works, accordingly, he took care to be illogical."[25] These private papers reveal that he was almost persuaded by the logic of naturalistic ontological monism (Spinozism)[26] but shrank back, finding it threatening to the immortality of the soul, the doctrine of the Trinity, theistic morality, and theodicy. CK seems to have the same problem at least with regard to the theistic morality and theodicy. CK abandon their ostensible monism ("anomalous" "emergent" or otherwise) by postulating that "emergent complexity" will give them gratis hierarchical "levels" of physical, mental, and spiritual each of which have their own sets of causal properties, *implying that these are separable*. What they advocate *de facto* is a metaphysical substance pluralism like Leibniz but without saying so in *Predicament*.

The "causal closure of the physical world" is simply "the seamlessness of natural explanation" (58), which means that the universe is causally seamless, such that every effect emerges from efficient causes. This does not require that "the total amount of energy in the universe is fixed" (55), that is, a thermodynamically closed system. We do not know if our observable universe is thermodynamically open or closed and there's no empirical reason to think seamless causality inconsistent with either option, so we won't discuss it further here, except to note that seamless causality is important in a NEO-consistent world. Where we fully agree is that "reductionist philosophies of science are not able to tell the whole story of scientific knowledge" (56). Reductionism derives from the old paradigm of a mechanical materialism (see note 18). Modern science without contradiction uses methods both reductive and systems-based. We all agree that they are not mutually exclusive but both indispensable to a healthy scientific enterprise. Each are methodological with their strengths and limitations.

Also, we strongly agree that "it just isn't true that the whole story can be told in neurological terms" (57). Neurons or molecules as minimal components *on their own* are not all there is to our experienced mental life. *The scientific evidence is overwhelming that mental life is inextricably and intrinsically neurological, bound up causally with dynamic and causal states of networks of neurons, in turn bound up with dynamic molecular systems, down to the quantum level, as well as up to the higher dynamic social group, community, habitat, and ecosystem levels,* whatever else we may speculate or desire. The entire contingent, multi-directional causal "hairball" was and is necessary to evolve and generate the lived experience of mental life. Billions of data points support upward and downward causal *inseparability,* and none are opposing.

Metaphysical fears? So, like Leibniz, Kant, Schelling, and others, from what are CK fleeing, even while they try to embrace it in a qualified form (anomalous monism or panentheism)? Throughout the history of thought the developing ideas of Democritus, Epicurus, Lucretius, Averroes/Ibn Rushd, Bruno, or Spinoza were feared as subversive and heretical. These heretics and mystics were groping toward the same reality that other great religious mystics in many traditions also espied: *the immanent infinity and unity of existence.* There is something terrifying in the simplicity, grandeur, and almost overwhelming self-evidence of the idea that there *ultimately* lurks intimately beneath everything *only one immanent infinite and creative reality, with its intrinsic mathematical rules of cause-effect, of which we and everything that is are finite elements.*[27] Whatever cosmology turns out to better approximate reality, whether yet another variation of the ΛCDM big bang, an oscillatory universe, inflationary universes in some multiverse, with expanding bubble universes as common as dandelions in spring, or some other more accurate model—all worlds would be mere modes of that one unified infinity. Whatever biological, organismal, ecological, and social complexities emerge, would all be causally intrinsic in this one immanent infinite reality in numerous interacting causal interchanges. The immanent oneness of infinite reality glimpsed by great non-religious as well as religious thinkers in every great religious tradition for centuries has a leveling effect on human pretensions and private worlds of illusion, whether of national glory, tribal privilege, ethnic superiority, in-group claims to divine favor or election, parochial theologies, or personal egocentric importance. The mystics and heretics were glimpsing the same one Reality. CK need not fear this, as we shall argue below.

Sole aims. CK close their discussion of science by stating that their "sole aim here has been to show that the realm of the mental represents at least one natural sphere in which divine action can occur, without overriding the regularities whose preservation is a necessary condition for the emergence of finite rational agents" (59). Their argument culminating in this "sole aim" seems (1) to reserve one area of the universe, the human brain, where God may still intervene to alleviate suffering without technically violating the NEO principle, thus an Irenaean world capable of the evolution of moral agents. And (2) to preserve human freedom from a reductionist "mechanical materialism" and it's resulting "determinism." Human freedom does not require any divorce from natural causation (see Appended Note).

The journey into science and its frontiers helps but little because the personal theistic problem of suffering and evil remains moral, not scientific. And nothing from the scientific investigation of the universe provides exemptions to the NEO principle. And even if exemptions existed, that is no excuse in a demonstrably unfair world.

"Does the Problem of Evil Now Return in a New Form?" (59)

Suppose that the mental is not governed by natural causation, ignoring the violation of the not-even-once principle. CK ask whether the problem of evil is really solved if God can intervene in the minds of people? For example, couldn't he have communicated a warning to those in the path of the December 2004 tsunami without altering the course of nature? Wouldn't God then be under moral obligation to intervene in every case where such intervention could make a better outcome? Or is divine thought so high above human thought that no communication is possible? Recognizing that any intervening communication violates NEO and fairness, CK propose another theory.

Axiological participation theory. CK warn against over-anthropomorphizing God, and suggest that divine communication may be *axiological* in that God would present each individual with a "value" which they are free to embrace or reject. In the *participatory theory of divine human agency*, there is a universal divine lure or attraction, not necessarily non-personal, with individuated appeals to every creature "which only becomes a definite message as it is interpreted and formulated by each recipient," leading to a "dialectical fusion of agency... accompanying them on their journeys, inspiring their joys, and luring them, gently, into harmony with the divine will" (64-65). This participatory model has God "involved in every instance of human action and experience in ways that infinitely exceed our comprehension.... [In] self-giving love...God participates with a[n]... intimacy that, once again, exceeds our imagination" (65-66). In short, God is involved and suffers more than anyone. Again, the problem for theodicy is that any participatory "lure" and capacity to respond are not fairly distributed. Also, there is still no solution for those disasters outside the control of human agency, because "such a God may not be able to stop a fatal mudslide, or warn the villagers" (65) in it's path.

What about the ethics of God luring creatures subconsciously and unevenly?[28] Is the "lure" influence distinguishable from the evolutionary selection for adaptive thriving and flourishing, eusocial reciprocity, and biological empathy? Such a lure seems indistinguishable from our innate biological empathy, evolved eusociality, and conscience: "We are not alone in the universe. We have each other."[29] But where is the justice in a non-egalitarian personal lure? Isn't a personal God still inevitably showing favoritism? Whatever befalls sentient beings for good or ill is not distributed evenly, but "time and chance happens to all" (Eccl. 9:11).

Are any of these attempts really a solution, whether or not in violation of the NEO principle? The world is empirically unfair. Do these attempts justify the misery of the smallest, uncomprehending creature? CK reference a dialogue in Dostoyevsky's *Brothers Karamazov*; when Alyosha is asked whether he would agree to the torture to death of one tiny baby to insure future human happiness, he replies, "No, I wouldn't consent."[30] Among social animals the reciprocal altruistic signaling to avoid conflict or secure favors can become costly. When misdirected by humans toward invisible "beings" and "deities" the cost of placation without reciprocation can become unhinged—the desperate logic and horrific results of human sacrifice and forms of self-immolation appear in human (pre-)history, in almost every religious tradition, including Christianity.

For CK, the problem of suffering and evil returns with a vengeance. There is no evidence that the mental is beyond natural causation, and the data overwhelmingly show that it isn't. But even if the mental were claimed to be exempt from natural causation, the problem persists, the same as if God were claimed to intervene regularly in nature. The *Tetralemma* of Epicurus endures, but a "lure" toward the moral comprises common ground, however unfair the world.

Mortality and "the Eschatological Dimension" (66)

CK respond to the second part of the "argument from neglect" asking, what if Wildman's objection is correct and there is no personal God? Does theism have moral relevance in its non-personal form? At a minimum, argue CK, the moral relevancy of non-personal theism would be confined, to those who "already, as the Gospel saying goes, 'have their reward'" (66). Mortalism is the position that death is the end of personal existence, a natural, regenerative part of life.[31] Many of the greatest thinkers in history were mortalists, as were some of the Bible writers. Life does not become less precious or devoid of happiness because it is passing, but rather the opposite, because life encompasses far more than our individual egos. Generations of large stars lived and perished in fiery explosions yielding the elements for life and planets such as Earth. Species went extinct, leaving ecological niches for new species. Generations have offspring, and then pass on leaving the next generation. This process can be viewed as self-giving, as kenotic. Our individual lives, whether selfish or shining outward with love, are all we give back to the universe which through our ancestors gave us being. Facing personal mortality with dignity and unselfishness is a fitting epitaph on a life well-lived.

If God is non-personal, they say, "then suffering in this life, and indeed the fate of the vast majority of all human beings who have ever lived, is unredeemed and unredeemable, and their hope is not only false but cruel. There can be no hope of any future consummation" (66). Exactly what, they ask, is "the moral contribution of such despair to 'the practical moral struggles of our deeply unjust world'?" CK charge that to question theodicy under "such despair" is to commit an *ad hominem tu quoque* (appeal to hypocrisy).[32] No. It's *not* the critic who acquits a personal deity of all responsibility for "our deeply unjust world" by appealing to an unknown afterlife. On the contrary, linking theodicy to an afterlife and morality to future reward or punishment, is probably *the* ethical low point of person-language theism. CK agree that it is moral immaturity to see a zero-sum between an afterlife and cheap hedonism, "Eat, drink, and be merry, for tomorrow we die." A moral person lives thus because it is right, not because of postmortem pay-off or payback.[33] The moral imperative of "our deeply unjust world" is to fight for a freer, happier life for others and to alleviate their life-suffering now. And that imperative rests urgently upon us today as mortals—not as immortals in waiting.[34]

The "hope of eschatological fulfillment," according to Wildman, raises the problem of God being "morally inconsistent" across all "cosmological epochs" (66). In response, CK assert that God's ultimate purpose across all epochs is creating moral agents to respond to his love. "In short, it is perfectly possible for God to create other and better worlds without contradicting what, on our hypothesis, was God's purpose in creating this one. And that hypothesis, we submit, provides a sufficiently plausible answer to the argument from neglect" (68). *Hoc non est quod demonstrandum erat*—Nothing is demonstrated! To the upturned, tear-stained little face of a hurting child, what kind of answer is that? It's all better—somewhere else! The *Tetralemma* of Epicurus remains.[35]

Reflections on the Ultimate

CK's preferred theology is panentheism[36] —God envelopes and is other than the world. In *Adventures in the Spirit* (2008), Clayton's preferred metaphysics is Arthur Peacock's *emergent monism*, in which the universe is *neither* physical nor mental, *nor* simultaneously both, but rather exists on different levels chronologically and then simultaneously—as pointed out, substance pluralism, not monism at all. Literature on the venerable tradition of panentheism, including Clayton's co-authored and co-edited works (2004, 2014), shows that panentheists seem to lapse back toward dualism, frequently juxtaposing "matter" and "spirit" and kindred concepts as ontological dualities.[37] If human mental properties emerge from the physical complexity of the brain and central nervous system, why not have God emerge from the cosmos as in *radically emergent theism*? According to Clayton, this is not desirable nor logically compelled "because" his task is to find an emergent theology which is consistent with an emergent "downward causal" view of agency and "adequate to the Christian tradition" where God pre-exists the world.[38] He proposes a *moderately emergent theism* (akin to process theology) in which God has two natures—one antecedent and one consequent.

No analogies for the ultimate. CK see personhood, mind, and agency as "higher order properties," therefore God must be a person.[39] This seems to be thinly disguised anthropocentrism. Other than the human need to relate to a person, why would God be analogous to a human person, since an ecosystem of persons, or the entire biosphere of a living planet like Earth, which contains humans, is that much more complex and grand? Why not make a planetary biosphere an analogy for divinity, or an inhabited galaxy of millions of interacting intelligent life-containing planets, or better yet, the entire universe? Why use the highly provisional individually focused consciousness as an analogy for an infinite divine "awareness" or "unconsciousness"? Best yet, why use analogies at all?

Analogical conceptions of the ultimate are unnecessary. Consider the *Tao Te Ching* (道德經, sixth century BCE), Part 7:[40]

> The Tao is infinite, eternal.
> Why is it eternal?
> It was never born;
> Thus it can never die.
> Why is it infinite?
> It has no desires for itself;
> Thus it is present for all beings.

The *Tao Te Ching* and other traditions in the East as well as the best thought in the Western traditions expose at least two significant errors of personalistic theism. (1) *Loss of infinity*—Personhood, agency, mind, consciousness, subjectivity, desires, loves, hates, preferences, jealousies, yearning for praise, hopes and dreams are all in the nature of a finite, bounded being who can contemplate what is outside and beyond itself. *The immanent nature of the infinite encompasses the all.* Postulating God as a personal agent choosing the particular laws of Nature makes God finite by placing Godself within, a subset of infinity. If God is an agent choosing among possible universes, fine-tuning or intervening, then both God and the universe would be contained within in a still-larger universe of those possibilities—God would be neither infinite nor unique—and so on *ad infinitum*.[41] Reifying human characteristics, proximal and provisional as they are, as divine, ultimately reduces the divine. That is the second error of personalistic theism, one familiar in terminology to monotheists: (2) *idolatry*—setting up human conceptions as worthy of worship.[42]

This idolatry is exposed by the universe unveiled by science, as Carl Sagan and others have pointed out, "A general problem with much of Western theology in my view is that the god portrayed is too small. It is a god of a tiny world [actually starting as a very tribal clan deity] and not a god of a galaxy much less of a universe."[43] "The gods of the human primate from this little blue planet.... are too small and petty for the grandeur of the stars and universe. Human gods do not even cover the scale of the earth and its history much less the universe."[44]

In the West, many and competing conceptions of even the one God of monotheism, some with a horrific record of dogmatism, cruelty, and superstition, have evolved and disappeared with cultural, political, and other historical processes.[45] CK love science and seek a rational religious faith with a moral conception of divinity. They are to be thanked for that effort and would do well to go further and set aside the inadequate idolatries of western theological thought, however "orthodox" and sacralized by long ecclesiastical tradition they may be. The liberal and radical theologies have more daring insight: (1) God could have given birth to the universe, and kenotically died in childbirth, leaving the universe on its own (cf. Kabbalah). (2) In creating the universe, God could have become a shade, a scarcely real shadow of Godself, powerless and fading, as Loren Eiseley poetically suggested, "God himself may rove in similar pain up the dark roads of his universe."[46] (3) God could becoming, an unfolding realization, as in radically-emergent theism or in the "omega" theologies of Teilhard de Chardin and Frank Tipler. (4) God could be the antecedent and consequent deity of process theology as in Alfred N. Whitehead. (5) Over the last three centuries with the Scientific Revolution, "death of god" thinkers and theothanatologists have contemplated the possibility that "God is dead" in some sense. These broadly include, among others, William Blake, Georg W. F. Hegel,

Frederich Nietzsche, Paul Tillich, Thomas Altizer, and Slavoj Žižek.[47] (5) CK's own tradition of panentheism tries to make sense of our world by enveloping it in God.

The limitation of every theology is that they are all human-made conceptions and yes, sublimations of our own deepest hopes, wishes, and contradictions.[48] And the weakness of all theologies, is that "they're asking all the questions except the one that matters: *Is any of this true?*"[49] The burden of any claim remains with the claimant, particularly for moral claims. *Quod gratis asseritur, gratis negatur* goes the old Latin proverb,[50] well-paraphrased in Hitchen's Razor: "What can be asserted without evidence can also be dismissed without evidence."[51] Dismissing unfounded claims does not mean that there is no infinite *substance*, no Tillichean "ground of being," no God or ultimate reality, but an important step toward finding that ultimate.

A summing up. In the end, we are left with a stark reality. Human-constructed deities, are not up to the task of resolving the problem of suffering—they cannot pass a parental responsibility test:

- In the world, in sentient beings, there exists drastic injustice, unfairness, and suffering, as well as goodness, happiness, and even justice. These stubborn facts, unevenly distributed, do not go away.
- Emergent complexity, biological agency, and downward causation are observed phenomena emerging naturally within a unified (monistic) world—requiring neither extraneous partial monism, substance pluralism, nor panentheistic dualism.
- Appeals to violations of the NEO principle (self-imposed but then disputed in CK's theology) are vacuous on scientific, logical, and moral grounds. CK should not abandon NEO, even in the human mind.

- The evolution of deep (axiological) values of bio-empathy and eusocial reciprocity in sentient beings—whether or not co-experienced as a "lure" by them and a world-enveloping spirit—does not change that life is drastically unfair or that natural disasters occur beyond the control of finite minds.
- Nothing exempts a moral agent from moral action, whether conceived as a deity or not. Thoughtful humans have long known the answer to Euthyphro's question in Plato's *Dialogues: The gods must do right because it is right,* not because they are gods. No gods ever conceived by humankind are exempt from the parameters of the universe, whether causal or moral. Reality is greater than all the gods.
- Science is learning to repent of the confident, even dogmatic reductionism of its youthful exuberance, and must now soberly face the reality of complexity, emergence, and systems dynamics. Through greed and misuse of technology, we have polluted our planet and harmed fellow Earthlings. Religion needs to repent of multiplying god conceptions with their theologies, all too often dogmatic, fanatical, and superstitious, thus imposing miseries on humankind, and enabling planetary pollution and habitat destruction.
- Not only heretics and mystics, but philosophers, mathematicians, scientists, artists, and others more than ever have opportunity to contemplate the infinite,[52] and embrace our duty to each other.

Anthropodicy

Suppose the great human questions as "Why suffering?" and "What is life's meaning?" are addressed to us. Auschwitz survivor, existentialist, and psychiatrist, Viktor Frankl wrote, "Ultimately, man should not ask what the meaning of his life is, but rather he must recognize that it is *he* who is asked. In a word, each man is questioned by life; and he can only answer to life by *answering for* his own life; to life he can only respond by being responsible."[53]

The universe in its stark beauty and vastness seems to have no answers *for us, apart from us*. From our evolutionarily-favored sociality and biological empathy, the only answer is *ours to give—action to relieve suffering and bring happiness to our fellow creatures*—to heal our collapsing ecosystems through habitat restoration, to birth new planetary life-friendly democratic economic systems, and to establish justice and freedom for our fellow Earthlings. Anthropodicy puts the onus on us—*we* must answer the world's suffering with our love—our empathy in action, what Jesus might have called, "the kingdom of God." The hour is late. With CK, we unite for joint life-saving action with people of conscience in every community and religious tradition, among religious naturalists and the more secular. Morals and world-views are shifting toward reality. We stand at a future-defining existential moment. Will we succeed in time? To live together responsibly in the great interconnected web of mutual reciprocity, would entail a participatory conception of the divine, a *telos* worthy of our best and of the immanent, infinite reality of it all.

On the other hand, to invent theodicies, whether by appeal to God's inscrutable purposes, to painful divine tests, to free will, to happy endings, or to benign neglect, is as intellectually unsatisfactory as it has been fruitless. Worse yet, theodicy-making may be not only immature but ultimately immoral. Theodicy-making justifies and prolongs suffering, and gives excuses for tyranny and oppression, as it has for centuries. It places on a deity what is our responsibility. The real dignity of humankind is moral adulthood.

Appended Note on Human Freedom[54]

In lectures on religious naturalism (2007), Wesley Wildman[55] argues that there is an emerging strategic consensus in the science and philosophy of mind. Neither mind-body dualism, immaterial idealism, eliminative materialism nor epiphenomenalism are adequate to the complex data of human consciousness and behavior, including religious and spiritual experiences (RSEs). Instead the emerging consensus now is *di-polar monism*: "One kind of basic stuff with mental and material aspects." Three and a half centuries after the fact, that is Spinozism, except that Spinoza considered the attributes of "thought" and "extension" to be the only two attributes of infinite *substance* humans can perceive, out of an infinite number of divine attributes.

When Baruch de Spinoza, the son of a Portuguese *marrano* whose community had fled the Portuguese Inquisition to Amsterdam, was growing up, the Scientific Revolution was underway. As Augustine's bloodied "city of God," Medieval Christendom, was crumbling with the ending of the devastating religious Thirty Years War (1648), young "Bento" was thrown out of the synagogue for talking in strange ways about God or Nature. Choosing a new name, Benedict de Spinoza chose to live neither as Jew nor Christian but as a free man. Together with other dissenters first in the Dutch Republic, he became a founder of the Radical Enlightenment. Neither Descartes (dualism), Hobbes (early mechanical materialism), Leibniz (pluralism), nor Berkeley and Kant (idealism), from Enlightenment times have been as productive of ongoing questions in speculative philosophy, mathematics, neuroscience, psychology, and even the foundations of modern physics as has Spinoza (monism). One of the controversies over ontological monism since the Enlightenment is the question of determinism and free will.

A striking breakthrough on human freedom came in the mid-twentieth century with a young philosophy graduate, novelist, playwright, and later French *Resistance* fighter against Nazi occupation, Jean-Paul Sartre. Sartre was in rebellion against, yet deeply influenced by, the legacy of the Hegelian dialectic of German Idealism in the phenomenology of Edmund Husserl and by the existential views of Kierkegaard and Heidegger. During a few months in a Nazi camp, Sartre considered freedom in action phenomenologically. Once outside, he joined the French *Resistance* and rapidly wrote a major work, *Being and Nothingness* (1943).[56] A passionate critic of power both West and East through plays and other writings, he became one of the most influential of twentieth century thinkers. Three centuries apart, Spinoza and Sartre contributed to the question of human freedom.

Causal inseparability from the universe and human freedom? Grant all the scientific evidence that the physical causalities of the universe fully operate in the human brain. Then, all known brain and nervous system activities are causally-embedded in the universe, from the single membrane crossing of one sodium ion to the discordant neuron-firing of a *grande mal* seizure, to the intense activation of certain brain regions by beautiful music, profound wonder, grief, laughter, sexual arousal, or agonizing decisions, or the loss of some neural activity in sociopaths, and even the emergent interaction of many brains in social ecosystems. Also there is the genetic and epigenetic expression effecting and pre-dispositioning the brain and nervous system, personality, emotional outlook, and addictability. Are humans left unfree in any practical sense that matters for human wellbeing? No. So how can we still affirm human freedom?

Ontological monism. Objectively, like all living things, humans are causally-inseparable parts and products of Nature (Spinoza). So, "every human action must be conceived of as a manifestation of nature,"[57] specifically the nature of humans, mammals, vertebrates, animals, etc. Thus, every process in our behavior can be traced to efficient natural causes with "consistent" discoverable "causal closure," but yet "in an intrinsically-contingent way" rather than a "fixed" algorithmic process.[58] How? Being modal parts of Nature, *humans simultaneously model Nature and self-model through a recursive process of incomplete approximations of the world in and around them via sensory input, reflective perception and semiotic interpretation.* This self-recursion is always incomplete, tentative, and contingent, under constant update by data from the "unobservable processes actually taking place"[59] within us and beyond. The diverse results of this recursive modeling by sentient beings (including humans) are objectively observed and *are* biological agency or freedom. Biological freedom can be objectively observed at different levels: (1) the creativity of solitary and social biological agents in environment-altering and self-transformation, and (2) the long term evolution of populations into new species adapting to almost every conceivable circumstance and environment. Life invents.[60] And in biological agents, there are "teleodynamic" downward causal changes. Objectively, the causal degree of complexity of the inventional behavior (solitary or social) is directly proportional to the "neural network connections" from the slightest "irritability" in microbes to the most complex sentient beings. Next we consider the subjective experience of freedom.

Existential and phenomenological. Subjectively, the recursive (self-) modeling of Nature *is itself* sentience, awareness, consciousness—*a finite (semiotic) representation of the world entailing a self-representation.* The world is what is, sheer facticity—"being-in-itself" (Sartre). Fragile and contingent, "consciousness is born supported by a being which is not itself."[61] This finite recursive (self-)representational "awareness" is causally-inseparable, with no real "distance" from the biological being. Hence, consciousness is the gaze "from nowhere," a "nothingness," "not a thing" or an object, but a *subject*, a "for-itself / for-others," which is an "awakeness" or "presence" to being-in-itself, the facticity of the world. Finite recursive (self-)representation opens wide the possibilities of *negation—(self-)representation of things as they are not*, that is, an *intention* for things to be other than they are—a restless, never satisfied, intention-oriented process. That subjective awareness is not an ontological being but a "becoming" with "nothing" to prevent its continual self-invention. Thus, though causally-inseparable from the world, the finite, recursive "we" as *subjects* are free because we cannot be other than free. We are "thrown into the world," "condemned to be free," and "forlorn" with the angst of inescapably having to choose, to invent, to actualize, to commit, to make sense and find meaning. Our finite (self-) representations involve the "nothingness" of *negation*: What was but is no more (nostalgia), what might have been (regret, wistfulness), what may yet be (hopes, dreams, foreboding), what can never be (longing, despair), what is and why (sense-making, meaning-making, world-view making), and what is beyond our limits (the infinite). Sentient (self-)representational beings may interact empathically with semiotic reciprocity (an intersubjectivity of goodness, beauty, love), treat other sentients as "objects" mere assets to an end, or with reciprocal spite (an intersubjectivity of evil, exploitation, revenge). From this "nothingness" of freedom arises the heights of creative art, innovation, discovery, or the depths of self-deception (*mauvais fois,* bad faith)—the agony and ecstasy of the entire human moral universe.

Ontological monism and science. Therefore, causally embedded in the universe, as finite (self-) modelers of Nature we construct world-models. Uniting systematic observation, reason, and mathematics, we apprehend aspects of the world by means of infinity (*substance*). This includes both the vastly large and the infinitesimal through the behavior and properties of what exists in spatial-temporal dimensionality (*extension*) and the logical entailment (*thought*) of applying mathematics with the infinities of real numbers, complex numbers, topologies, and various algebras. Thus linking the directly mappable correspondences between physical and mathematical properties and behaviors we can make rigorous, testable theories—from quantum electrodynamics to general relativity to game theory to population genetics. By means of our systematic, mathematical, recursive (self-)modeling of Nature, we begin to glimpse universal, unified causality—logical entailment where "thought is co-extensive with materiality."[62] *Ordo et connexio idearum idem, est ac ordo et connexio rerum*: "The order and connection of ideas corresponds to the order and connection of things,"[63] i.e., in mathematical terms, a mappable correspondence. Nature contains and is immanent, so that finite, (self-)representational modelers through observation and thought may apprehend attributes of the infinite: "Thinking substance and extended substance are one and the same substance, comprehended now under this attribute, now under that.... [That is, both] in God—are one and the same thing, explicated through different attributes." From a universal perspective, the converse equivalent holds: Infinite *substance* is distributively structured "in terms of infinitely many self-representations, one of which is our" observable universe.[64] Infinite, unified, atemporal, undifferentiated *substance* is indistinguishable from the infinite non-being of the potential and the possible, and modally actualized in *what has become*—what is finite, modal, and temporal.[65] In short, if temporality only arises in the transition from the infinite to the modal (human) perspective,[66] even on those terms (momentarily setting aside the subjective, phenomenological, and existential) is there "still a problem of determinism"?[67] It is worth noting in this context that Whiteheadian process conceptions of the divine are in danger of attempting to absolutize the finite, but that is another topic.

---

[1] The main strands of thought in conflict during the Enlightenment era were radical, moderate-conservative, and counter-Enlightenment, as described by Jonathan Israel in his massive multi-volume histories: *Radical Enlightenment: Philosophy and the Making of Modernity, 1650-1750* (Cambridge: Cambridge University Press, 2001); *Enlightenment Contested: Philosophy, Modernity, and the Emancipation of Man 1670-1752* (Cambridge: Cambridge University Press, 2006); *Democratic Enlightenment: Philosophy, Revolution, and Human Rights 1750-1790* (Cambridge: Cambridge University Press, 2011), and *Revolutionary Ideas: An intellectual history of the French Revolution from* The Rights of Man *to* Robespierre (Princeton: Princeton University Press; 2014).

[2] Among Leibniz' many accomplishments was the independent co-discovery of the calculus with Sir Isaac Newton.

[3] Originally published in 1710, the French version of the theodicy of Gottfried Leibniz was *Essais de Théodicée sur la Bonté de Dieu, la Liberté de l'Homme et l'Origine du Mal* (Amsterdam: Changuion, 1734), which in English is *Essays of Theodicy on the Goodness of God, the Freedom of Man and the Origin of Evil.* See Austin Farrer, *Introduction to the* Theodicy (La Salle: Open Court, 1985). The work is also called *Théodicée* for short.

[4] See http://www.philosophy-index.com/terms/dike.php, and the "theodicy"entry in Wikipedia.

[5] See Thom Stark's *The Human Faces of God: What Scripture Reveals When It Gets God Wrong (And Why Inerrancy Tries to Hide It)*, (Eugene: Wipf and Stock Publishers, 2011). The Christian New Testament is not exempt because of predestination and hell. Particularly the Pauline and Johannine writings have a recurring appeal to predestination and damnation, although ameliorated in part over the centuries by Pelagian, semi-Pelagian, Arminian, and universalist currents in Christianity. Furthermore, there are a growing number of conservative Christian thinkers who are abandoning the old notion of an eternal hell of torment: Edward W. Fudge, *The Fire that Consumes: A Biblical and Historical Study of the Doctrine of Final Punishment*, third edition, (Eugene: Cascade Books, 2011); *Rethinking Hell: Readings in Evangelical Conditionalism* eds. Christopher I. Date, Gregory M. Stump, Joshua W. Anderson (Eugene: Cascade Books, 2014).

[6] John W. Loftus, "The Darwinian Problem of Evil" (chapter 9), *The Christian Delusion: Why Faith Fails*, ed. John W. Loftus (Amherst: Prometheus Books, 2010).

[7] Albert Camus, *L'Étranger* (1942); *The Stranger*, trans. Stuart Gilbert, (New York: Alfred A. Knopf, 1946), Part II, ch. 5.

[8] Bart D. Ehrman, *God's Problem: How the Bible Fails to Answer Our Most Important Question—Why We Suffer* (San Francisco: Harper Collins, 2008).

[9] Wesley J. Wildman, "A Review and Critique of the 'Divine Action Project': A Dialogue among Scientists and Theologians Sponsored by Pope John Paul II," Unpublished manuscript (n.d.), 3. Cited in *Predicament*, chapter 3.

[10] A concept more prominent since the Nazi Holocaust (millions of deaths, aside from war casualties, of Jews, Gypsies, gays, socialists, unionists, Slavs; including the Nazi-satellite Ustazi Croat genocide of Serbs, Jews, and Gypsies) while certain leaders of the Christian churches, of Allied governments, and of business and finance, mostly stood by and/or abetted either financially or otherwise. Similar complicities are found with the Tibetan, Cambodian, Indonesian, and Rwandan genocides, etc. Any theodicy must face the challenge of bystander guilt.

[11] It is important to note that the application of the notion of "laws" in regard to the causal patterns of nature is always metaphorical.

[12] Freiherr von Gottfried Wilhelm Leibniz, *Theodicy: Essays on the Goodness of God, the Freedom of Man, and the Origin of Evil*, ed. Austin Farrer, trans. E. M. Huggard (Charleston: BiblioBazaar, 2007), 364: 393.

[13] Peter A. Corning, "The Re-emergence of 'Emergence': A Venerable Concept in Search of a Theory," *Complexity* 7, no. 6 (2006): 18–30.

[14] Peter A. Corning (2012). "The Re-emergence of Emergence, and the Causal Role of Synergy in Emergent Evolution." *Synthese* 185, no. 2 (2012): 295–317. See the broad range of work connected with the Institute for the Study of Complex Systems (www.complexsystems.org), the Sante Fe Institute (www.santafe.edu), and the multi-volume sets of studies of emergent and complex phenomena and the journal *Emergence: Complexity & Organization An International Transdisciplinary Journal of Complex Social Systems* published by Emergent Publications, and in other scientific journals. The term "emergence" is often used in the social sciences, whereas the physical, biological sciences and artificial intelligence communities often use the terms self-organization and self-organizing complex systems.

[15] Corning, "The Re-emergence of 'Emergence'," (2002).

[16] "Teleodynamic" is the term used to describe biological teleological, purpose-driven, and goal-oriented behavior and mental phenomena by Terence Deacon, *Incomplete Nature: How Mind Emerged from Matter* (New York: W.W. Norton, 2011) and other references cited by CK. It is interesting that CK cite Deacon, Paul Davies, and other emergentists in defense of their own substance pluralism or even panentheistic dualism—positions apparently quite distinct from those of these scientists—who do not share the theological concerns or metaphysics of CK.

[17] "Anomalous monism" is a philosophical thesis about the mind-body

relationship first proposed by Donald Davidson (1970) and developed since. Donald Davidson, "Mental Events" in *Actions and Events* (Oxford: Clarendon Press, 1980).

[18] A common error in discussions about reductionism, determinism, and materialism (which CK seem to successfully avoid) is that science (knowledge) is often considered in terms of modern specialized disciplines, instead of the broadly "core epistemological categories" in their classic Stoic sense, where *physics* is the modeling of nature, *logic* is the modeling of reason (*logos*) and thinking in the context of nature, and *hermeneutics* is the modeling of thinking about thought. It is only in this broad classic sense that "the sciences are *reducible* to physics" and we include modern physics among the scientific disciplines "as a special case at their basic foundations" where mathematical modeling and empirical inference are most intimately linked. At the same instant, the "higher levels of complexity are *irreducible* to physics in the sense that by passing down the hierarchy, emergent properties are effectively being lost" in Ranier E. Zimmermann, "Loops and knots as *topoi* of substance: Spinoza revisited" (arXiv:gr-qc/0004077v2, 2000). These non-contradictory points, which should be obvious, are missed because some idealist or dualist / pluralist polemic is muddled by a focus on a pre-quantum, pre-relativistic, Newtonian-Laplacian "mechanical materialism" (late eighteenth to nineteenth centuries) and/or the "dialectic materialism" rooted in Marx and Engels (late 19th century), and developed in ideological blasts from the former Soviet Union (twentieth century). In short, at least some modern idealist and dualist / pluralist polemicists are still fighting a kind of philosophical Cold War—which from the standpoint of science is over. Here I'm indebted in part to mathematician and philosopher R. E. Zimmerman in his 2000 paper, and in *New Ethics Proved in Geometrical Order: Spinozist Reflexions on Evolutionary Systems*, Exploring Unity through Diversity, Volume 2 (Litchfield Park: Emergent Publications, 2010), chapter 1.

[19] Matthew Stewart, *The Courtier and the Heretic: Leibniz, Spinoza, and the Fate of God in the Modern World* (New York: Norton & Company, 2006), 278.

[20] Ibid., 278.

[21] David Hume, *A Treatise of Human Nature* (London: John Noon, 1738), 240–1.

[22] Chronicled in the new and massive ~2,800 pages of the four volume history of the European Enlightenment from 1650 to 1800 by Jonathan Israel (2001 through 2013). Israel starts with the early radical Enlightenment in the Dutch republic, traces the battle between the radical-democratic, the moderate-aristocratic, and the counter-Enlightenments across the continent, in Russia, and in the Americas. He traces the historical documents through the French Revolution, the *Rights of Man*, and ends with the counter-Enlightenment coup that brought Robespierre to power in 1793.

[23] Stewart, *The Courtier and the Heretic* (2006), 310: Leibniz and Spinoza may be thought of as archetypal human responses to modernity.

[24] Philip Clayton, *Adventures in the Spirit: God, World, Divine Action*.

(Minneapolis: Fortress Press, 2008).

[25] Bertrand Russell (1900). *The Philosophy of Leibniz*. (London: Routledge, 1992).

[26] Gottfried Leibniz made a furtive trip to meet Spinoza in the Hague in November of 1676—an unrecorded meeting of two of the titans of Western thought—discussed along with details of his struggles with Spinozism in Stewart, *The Courtier and the Heretic* (2006).

[27] Despite the nineteenth century work of Georg Cantor on infinite sets and cardinalities of infinities, and the immediate immanence in modern science and mathematics of actual infinities through the application of real, transcendental, complex, algebraic number analyses, the calculus, particularly through ordinary and partial differential equations, and the higher algebras, etc., (not to bypass the ubiquitous reminders of infinity requiring renormalization in quantum electrodynamics and so on), at least some of the NIODA apologists seem to be fleeing, from actual infinity and unity. In this they follow Thomas Aquinas, the late Medieval "orthodox" persecutors of Nicolas of Cusa and Giordano Bruno, and the seventeenth and eighteenth century pious censors and proscribers of Spinoza—the heretic who conceptually and qualitatively anticipated Cantor by conceiving as actual both modal manifestations of infinities and substantive unitary infinity as immanent and indivisible (see not only the *Ethics*, but Letter XII). As far as I can tell, this does not include Clayton / Knapp, but some NIODA apologists seem to flee actual infinity for theological reasons, to protect their "orthodox" and very finite deity. We know today that Cantor was directly influenced by Spinoza's conception of infinity. See Paolo Bussotti and Christian Tapp, "The influence of Spinoza's concept of infinity on Cantor's set theory," *Studies in History and Philosophy of Science* 40, no. 1 (2009): 25–35.

[28] Dialogue with fellow reviewer James Walters brought the specific questions in this paragraph to my attention.

[29] Attributed to humanist scholar Corliss Lamont.

[30] Fyodor Dostoevsky, *The Brothers Karamazov*, trans. R. Pevear and L. Volokhonsky (New York: Knopf, 1992).

[31] Beautiful popular and curricular work on the generative meaning of death has been done by liberal Christian Michael Dowd, *Thank God for Evolution: How the Marriage of Science and Religion will Transform your Life and our World* (New York: Viking, Penguin Group, 2008), chapter 3, cf. http://evolutionarychristianity.com/blog/thank-god-for-death-could-anything-be-more-sacred-more-necessary-more-real/; and by atheist science writer and spouse Connie Barlow (http://www.thegreatstory.org/death-programs.html).

[32] *Ad hominem tu quoque*, literally "attack the man [by querying] you too?" i.e., a "pot-calling-the-kettle-black"ism.

[33] Albert Einstein, in an address on "Science and religion" at the Princeton Theological Seminary, 19 May 1939; published in *Out of My Later Years* (New York: Philosophical Library, 1950), said: "....whoever has undergone

the intense experience of successful advances made in this domain [natural sciences or we might add, in philosophy, religion, or the arts] is moved by profound reverence for the rationality made manifest in existence. By way of the understanding he achieves *a far-reaching emancipation from the shackles of personal hopes and desires*, and thereby attains that humble attitude of mind toward the grandeur of reason incarnate in existence, and which, in its profoundest depths, is inaccessible to man. This attitude, however, appears to me to be religious, in the highest sense of the word" (emphasis added).

[34] Bertrand Russell, "A free man's worship," *Independent Review* (December, 1903), wrote eloquently of the mortalist moral imperative: "The life of Man is a long march through the night, surrounded by invisible foes, tortured by weariness and pain, towards a goal that few can hope to reach, and where none may tarry long. One by one, as they march, our comrades vanish from our sight, seized by the silent orders of omnipotent Death. Very brief is the time in which we can help them, in which their happiness or misery is decided. Be it ours to shed sunshine on their path, to lighten their sorrows by the balm of sympathy, to give them the pure joy of a never-tiring affection, to strengthen failing courage, to instil faith in hours of despair. Let us not weigh in grudging scales their merits and demerits, but let us think only of their need—of the sorrows, the difficulties, perhaps the blindnesses, that make the misery of their lives; let us remember that they are fellow-sufferers in the same darkness, actors in the same tragedy with ourselves. And so, when their day is over, when their good and their evil have become eternal by the immortality of the past, be it ours to feel that, where they suffered, where they failed, no deed of ours was the cause; but wherever a spark of the divine fire kindled in their hearts, we were ready with encouragement, with sympathy, with brave words in which high courage glowed."

[35] David Hume stated in eighteenth century terms what is still applicable to a traditional theology: "God's power is infinite. Whatever he wills is executed but neither man nor other animals is happy. Therefore he does not will their happiness. Epicurus's questions are yet unanswered." Cited in http://www.secularsites.freeuk.com/jonathan_miller_quotes.htm.

[36] Panentheism is not as alien to Hebrew Scriptural and New Testament thought as often imagined. That the Jewish wisdom tradition with Hellenistic Stoicism influenced later Jewish literature / cosmology, including some of the theology of Paul and most significantly the *logos* poem in John 1, has been well established in James D. G. Dunn's *Christology in the Making: A New Testament Inquiry Into the Origins of the Doctrine of the Incarnation*, second edition (Grand Rapids: Eerdmans, 1989)—a point completely missed by the neo-Platonist, post-Chalcedon, Trinitarian christologies.

[37] Philip Clayton, *In whom We Live and Move and Have our Being: Panentheistic Reflections on God's Presence* (Grand Rapids: Wm. B. Eerdmans, 2004); John W. Cooper, *Panentheism, the other God of the Philosophers: From Plato to the Present*

(Grand Rapids: Baker Academic, 2006); Loriliai Biernacki and Philip Clayton, *Panentheism across the World's Traditions* (Oxford: Oxford University Press, 2014).

[38] Clayton, *Adventures in the Spirit* (2008), 102.

[39] Ibid., 96.

[40] Full a full English text of the *Tao Te Ching*, see the translation by S. Mitchell (last updated 20 July 1995; http://academic.brooklyn.cuny.edu/core9/phalsall/texts/taote-v3.html#7; accessed 22 April 2012).

[41] For a discussion on this infinite regress in the context of the world-view of Leibniz, see Stewart, *The Courtier and the Heretic* (2006).

[42] Not known for understatement, Christopher Hitchens put it concisely, "Thus the mildest criticism of religion is also the most radical and devastating one: Religion is man-made." Hitchens, *God is Not Great: How Religion Poisons Everything* (New York: Twelve, Hatchette Book Group, 2007), 10.

[43] Carl Sagan, *The Varieties of Scientific Experience: A Personal View of the Search for God*, 1985 Gifford lectures, ed. Ann Druyan (New York: Penguin Group, 2006), 30.

[44] From "To be Steeped in Natural History," http://www.pangeaprogress.com/blog/to-be-steeped-in-natural-history. The philosopher George Santayana is also apt in his rejection of such idolatry: "My atheism, like that of Spinoza, is true piety towards the universe and denies only gods fashioned by men in their own image, to be servants of their human interests," *Soliloquies in England and Later Soliloquies* (New York: Charles Scribner & Sons, 1922), 246.

[45] See the classic work of Karen Armstrong, *A History of God: The 4,000-year Quest of Judaism, Christianity, and Islam* (New York: Alfred A. Knopf, 1994).

[46] Loren Eiseley, *The Firmament of Time* (New York: Atheneum, 1960), 166, where he continues, "Only how would it be, I wonder, to contain at once both the beginning and the end, and to hear, in helplessness perhaps, the fall of worlds in the night?"—an unvarnished poetry of the problem of suffering and disaster. A kindred evocative poetic possibility (however unorthodox) is that a lonely deity is struggling in a universe beset by recurrent disaster and is in need of the forgiveness of the creatures of the universe.

[47] The "death of god" or *theothanatology*, whether envisaged by mystics, radical theologians, or secular philosophers, is an underestimated and re-emergent trend in Western thought ever since the Scientific Revolution and the early Enlightenment, with links to earlier mystics and their experience of the cosmic void or non-being; The first theothanatologist of the modern era was Christian mystic William Blake in the 1780s-90s. See Thomas J.J. Altizer, "William Blake and the Role of Myth in the Radical Christian Vision" in T. J. J. Altizer, William Hamilton, *Radical Theology and the Death of God* (Indianapolis: Bobbs-Merrill, 1966). Note also Richard L. Rubenstein, "God After the Death of God" in *After Auschwitz: History, Theology, and Contemporary Judaism*, second edition (Baltimore: Johns Hopkins University Press, 1992) 293–306. For a recent example, see Slavoj Žižek, *The Monstrosity of Christ: Paradox or Dialectic?* (Cambridge: MIT Press, 2009); And just published: Daniel J.

Peterson, G. Michael Zbaraschuk, Thomas J. J. Altizer, *Resurrecting the Death of God: The Origins, Influence, and Return of Radical Theology* (Albany: State University of New York Press, 2014).
[48] Sublimations "born of the refusal…to admit the cosmic darkness…. comforting illusions within the warm glow of which…to shelter…from the icy winds of the universe" according to Walter T. Stace (1948), *Man against Darkness and Other Essays* (Pittsburgh: University of Pittsburgh Press, 1967), 9.
[49] So queries a friend of mine, Steve Scianni, in pointing out the omission of this central theological question.
[50] Jon R. Stone, *The Routledge Dictionary of Latin Quotations: The Illiterati's Guide to Latin Maxims, Mottoes, Proverbs, and Sayings*, (New York: Routledge, 2005), 101.
[51] Hitchens, *God is Not Great* (2007), 150.
[52] As a practicing scientist, who also engages in meditation practice, I reach for the ultimate from both directions.
[53] Viktor E. Frankl (1959, 1962, 1984), *Man's Search for Meaning* (New York: Simon & Schuster, 1984), 131.
[54] Human freedom has traditionally been interpreted as the old metaphysical dualist "free will" conception which is at best untenable and even incoherent in light of advances today. Hence, I prefer the term human freedom, which preserves what people value about freedom, without using the old term "free will." Philosophy can still afford us a provisional framework for considering ultimate questions (*ultima philosophia*) such as human freedom, even though the Scientific Revolution has dethroned philosophy as *prima philosophia* in the Aristotelian sense. See Zimmermann, *New Ethics Proved* (2010), 5.
[55] Wesley J. Wildman, in a 6-part lecture series, "Religious Experiences: From the Mundane to the Anomalous," Center for the Study of Religion and Psychology, Danielsen Institute, Boston University (2007): https://www.youtube.com/watch?v=4j_lRGCt1pc.
[56] Jean-Paul Sartre, *L'Être et le Néant: Essai d'Ontologie Phénoménologique* (Paris, Gallimard, 1943). *Being and Nothingness: An Essay on Phenomenological Ontology*, transl. Hazel E. Barnes (New York: Philosophical Library, 1956).
[57] Don Garrett, "Spinoza's ethical theory" in *The Cambridge Companion to Spinoza*, ed. D. Garrett (Cambridge: Cambridge University Press, 1996), 267–314.
[58] Zimmermann, *New Ethics Proved* (2010), 10–11.
[59] Ibid., 5–6, 10–11.
[60] Biological agency or freedom or creativity is causally inseparable from but not reducible to a myriad facts in nature, some as lowly as the enormous possibilities of different chemical bonds because carbon has a valence of four with a medium electronegativity, or as striking as the relation that behavioral complexity varies directly with the neural complexity of the nervous system.
[61] From different standpoints these two philosophers provide a helpful heuristic framework for the modern philosophy of mind and the neurosciences. See Kathleen Wider, "Sartre and Spinoza on the Nature of Mind," *Continental*

Philosophy Review 46 (2013): 555–575; 560.

[62] Margaret D. Wilson, "Spinoza's theory of knowledge" in *The Cambridge Companion to Spinoza*, ed. Don Garrett (Cambridge: Cambridge University Press, 1996), 115.

[63] Benedict de Spinoza, in B. d. S., *Opera Postuma, Quorum Series Post Praefationem Exhibetur* (Amersterdam: Jan Rieuwertsz, 1677), Part II, Proposition VII. Rieuwertsz was the friend and book seller who secretly arranged the publication. (For a delightful annotated Internet English text from Elwes's translation of the *Ethics* including Spinoza's explanatory notes, see http://www.yesselman.com/e2elwes.htm#VII, part of a large website).

[64] Zimmermann, "Loops and Knots," 15.

[65] Ibid., 19. Compare Robert C. Neville's conception of non-being as indeterminate, and being as determinate, discussed in *Recovery of the Measure: Interpretation and Nature*, Axiology of Thinking, Vol. 2 (Albany: SUNY Press, 1989).

[66] W. Bartuschat, *Spinozas Theorie des Menschen* (Hamburg: Meiner, 1992), 85; Zimmermann, "Loops and Knots" (2000), 11.

[67] Zimmermann, "Loops and Knots" (2000), 11.

4

THE ULTIMATE REALITY: WHO AM I TO KNOW?

A Reflection on Chapter 4, "The Plurality of Religions"

Ervin Taylor

The principal issue considered by Clayton and Knapp (hereafter CK) in the relatively short fourth chapter of this volume concerns the implications of the empirical observation that human societies exhibit innumerable ways of framing the realm of what each society views as the mysterious or sacred. The same observation can be made about how human societies define the characteristics and activities of the entities (spirits, gods, or God) that are viewed as inhabiting these sacred realms and determine how humans are expected to interact with these sacred entities.

Ultimate Reality

The authors begin by reiterating their view of the realm of the sacred and the nature of the entity that inhabits sacred space. They characterize that entity using the term *ultimate reality* (UR), equating it with the traditional term "God." They restate their earlier assertion that their UR/God is "not *less* than personal" and exhibits "other-directed action in creation" that we humans might call "love." Their "hypothesis" about the nature of UR is captured by what they call *"minimally personalistic theism"* (MPT).

In an earlier chapter, they have responded to a challenge to their view of the nature of UR in light of the "problem of evil." Their "plausible explanation" of why UR does not intervene to prevent natural and man-made evils of various types is this: "God could not act, even once, in ways that would be incompatible with the regularities we call the laws of nature without becoming obligated to act in all cases where a similar good would be produced." However, their explanation allows "participatory" activities of UR, acting in humans in a manner that does not negate the "relative autonomy" of finite beings (69).

The authors state that their view of UR is "superior" (their term) to four other alternatives. These four alternatives are: (1) the universe is both eternal and necessary, i.e., it had no beginning and "it could not *not* have existed and hence it is self-explanatory"; (2) the universe is a "random quantum fluctuation in the void or some other entirely mindless and impersonal process"; (3) the universe is "the creation of a personal being…who happens to be either indifferent or hostile to finite persons and what matters to them"; and finally, (4) there is "simply no meaningful answer to the question of what is ultimately the case or why there is anything at all" (70).

They further argue that it makes "more sense" (again, their term) to suppose three things about the nature of UR. First, UR should be considered as a personal entity rather than an impersonal force. Second, UR should be conceived as "valuing the welfare of its finite creatures." Third, the UR would be "disposed to perform certain kinds of actions" so that "the universe [can]…sustain the evolutionary emergence of finite persons." They suggest that their assertions about the nature of the UR "are about as far as metaphysical reflection can go" (70).

They remind the reader that their hypothesis about the existence and nature of UR grows out of their considerations of the "metaphysical implications of contemporary science…[and specifically the question of] what kind of UR might have preceded the universe as a whole?" Within the context of a consideration of their hypothesis about the nature of UR, they suggest that there is a "major methodological break" that is *not* the transition to theism required by their hypothesis. They suggest that the actual break occurs "when one turns from theism in general to the specific historical and doctrinal beliefs of the individual religions" (70).

CK remind their readers that the religions of humanity advance "a number of different and (it would seem) not fully compatible ways of pinning down the…abstract content of MPT. The very fact that there are so many conflicting religious theories [about UR]…provides a powerful *prima facie* reason for doubting that any one of them is more likely to be true than false" (73). They further stipulate that their MPT concept "seems to offer insufficient reason to choose among the many religious options that potentially claim one's attention…in today's radically globalized religious environment" (71).

Taking into consideration all of the points raised earlier, the authors ask what conclusions can be drawn from the fact of "religious plurality," which is the title they assign to this chapter. They argue, citing John Hick, that "every religious theory [should be regarded] as a 'myth,' by which Hick means a particular story or narrative that human beings have developed to depict a reality that lies utterly beyond the reach of human knowledge" (74). Several other scholars reportedly argue that each religious system—or at least the major longstanding ones—

"capture a portion of a single truth that, in its totality, transcends the grasp of any particular tradition." Still others, including Alvin Plantinga, "admit the fact of religious plurality but deny its relevance, on the grounds that everyone is entitled to hold the beliefs she finds herself holding, unless [the individual] encounters unanswerable objections…" (74).

Finally, our authors argue that the set of alternatives by which one can consider the significance of religious pluralism exhibited by human societies seem to be just two. The first alternative is that "there is no answer (or at least no humanly accessible answer) to the question of which, if any, of the available religious alternatives best reflects the nature and intentions of the UR" (75). The proponents of the first option argue that "there is simply no way around the fact that each of us is trapped in, and indeed essentially blinded by, [our] religious and cultural milieu" (75). The second alternative says that the fact of religious pluralism is "irrelevant to the question of whether the theories embedded in one's own religious tradition are actually true…religious truth is no more affected by the existence of multiple religions than scientific truth is affected by the fact that people in earlier times believed that the earth was flat" (75). They insist that these alternatives can be characterized by a Latin phrase, *tertium non datur*, literally "third not given" which is a Latin idiom for "there are no other alternatives" (75).

Compliments and Concerns

My reflections on this chapter will be divided into compliments and concerns. Let us first consider the compliments:

The most helpful statement in the entire chapter is an observation that is certainly not original to the authors, but they have stated it in a compact and compelling manner. Because of its significance for the topic of this chapter, the statement is quoted in full:

> The very fact that there are so many conflicting religious theories, all purporting to describe the same UR, provides a powerful *prima facie* reason for doubting that any one of them is more likely to be true than false. Reasons for doubt intensify when one realizes that nearly all those who adhere to one religious tradition or another do so because that was the tradition in which they were raised or to which they were heavily exposed by the culture surrounding them. Moreover, each [religious] tradition provides its adherents with compelling experiences that naturally seem to them to confirm the truth of whatever religious theories the tradition may embody. (73)

The observations CK make in this paragraph contain three important elements.

All Religion is Relative

First, there is a "powerful *prima facie* reason" for asserting that, given the "many conflicting religious theories" of the past or present, any understanding or belief about the UR is more likely to be false than true. Second, this powerful reason is affirmed by the observation that it is most likely that "those who adhere to one religious tradition or another" embrace it because it was the one into which they were born and which is shared by anyone exposed to the same culture. It has little, if anything, to do with whether any particular, unique characteristic of that religious tradition is true—however "truth" might be determined. Third, each religious tradition "provides its adherents with compelling experiences that naturally seem to them to confirm the truth of whatever religious theories the tradition may embody."

These three observations significantly illumine the affect-saturated, emotionally compelling human attachment to the many particularistic, religiously inspired worldviews of believers. These attachments are particularly directed toward the deity or deity-like figure to which focused commitment is given. Not only do various modern religious systems provide a set of beliefs, practices, and cultural values that establish the boundaries for the definition of the community of like-minded individuals within which these beliefs and practices are exercised, but also these systems provide "compelling experiences" that validate one's religious beliefs and practices.

Well-known illustrations of this phenomenon in Western religious traditions include the "born again" experiences reported by many who actively participate within the Protestant evangelical and Pentecostal traditions, the "warm feelings" produced in adherents to the Mormon tradition to validate the Mormon theological system, and the "out-of-body" experiences (visions) of the Western Medieval mystics and even minor modern religious mystics such as the nineteenth-century American charismatic Ellen G. White. There are many more examples in many other traditions that testify to the validity and power of this observation of the authors.

My positive reaction to these particular assertions of the authors probably stems, in large part, from my academic background. The anthropological literature on worldviews and religious systems, particularly the literature on the concepts and practices exhibited in pre- or non-literate human societies, highlights the relevance of CK's observations. In fact, a widely-quoted definition of religion from a socio-cultural perspective, offered by the anthropologist Clifford Geertz, is entirely congruent with the focus of the authors' observations quoted above. This definition defines *religion* as consisting of a "system of symbols which acts to establish powerful, pervasive, and long-lasting moods and motivations in [humans] by formulating conceptions of a general order of existence and clothing these conceptions with such an aura of factuality that the moods and motivations [created by the system of symbols] seem uniquely realistic."[1]

A second major comment by the authors that I find very helpful is that for those formally educated within a contemporary Western European or American intellectual tradition, the most important "major methodological break" in considering any religious proposition is *not* to be found in the transition from theism to atheism. It is rather "when one turns from theism in general to the specific historical and doctrinal beliefs of the individual religions." In the context of the assertion of the authors that UR is not less than "personal," this suggestion is particularly pertinent. CK ask, "[W]here, if anywhere, in human history does one find signs of the presence and activity of an Ultimate Reality one has reason to regard as more like a personal agent than an impersonal force?" (71). The most straightforward answer would be that nowhere in human history does sufficient evidence exist to make such a declaration. Later, the authors state that "the choice among competing religious theories about the UR is *underdetermined*—left unresolved—by the arguments and evidence available to the community of inquiry as a whole" (71).

A third compliment concerns CK's term "Ultimate Reality" (UR), used in place of "God" as the semantic referent for the "ground of being" or that than which "no higher level of being can be conceived." The basis for my positive evaluation for this terminological substitution proceeds from a simple objection to the continuing use of *God/Gott/ Deus/Dios/Dieu/Dio*, or their linguistic equivalents in any language, in contemporary analytical discussions involving theological topics. "God" is a word that has lost essentially all of its usefulness as a meaningful analytical or descriptive linguistic symbol for many educated Western readers. I propose that for serious dialogue on this subject, "God" should be retired to some honored virtual museum of archaic words that can no longer carry the required or necessary conceptual content. An illustration of a term already residing in such a museum would be the "Earth-Fire-Water" phrase of ancient Greece, used as a means of describing the elements making up physical reality. I would understand if the authors of this work or others might think that I'm a bit naïve, since they might reasonably respond that nobody interested in this topic would worry about a mere word due to semantic baggage.

The Problem with "Personal"

The points noted above merit a positive response. However, other points in this chapter are problematical to various degrees.

The first arises from a consideration of two elements of a short sentence early in the chapter, which has already been noted. That sentence expresses CK's understanding that it makes *"more sense* [my emphasis] to suppose that the source and ground of all existence is an infinite reality more aptly described as *personal* [my emphasis] than impersonal" (70). The first part of this statement that seems highly questionable relates to the phrase "more sense." I unsuccessfully searched throughout the book for an explanation of the assertion that it makes "more sense" that UR is "personal."

It seems to me that, upon reading such a statement, the question naturally arises about what criterion or set of criteria one might reasonably use to decide if this statement makes "more sense." Making such an assertion would immediately raise a whole range of questions: to whom does it make more sense? In what context, using what system of logic, can one make such a determination? Who is in a position to make a determination whether this, or any assertion about such topics, makes more sense? Perhaps all of these points have been discussed elsewhere in the book and I failed to locate them. Or perhaps the authors assumed that anyone reading this chapter would have a common set of criteria for defining "more sense." This would be unlikely, since CK would certainly know that no such common frame of reference in the West has existed since at least the Enlightenment, and in the postmodern world no such category exists. In light of this, some readers will certainly question the degree to which their own view of the nature of UR makes "more sense."

The second highly problematic element in the statement quoted above is a key element of CK's argument in the first four chapters. This is the "hypothesis" that UR is both personal, or as they "would prefer to say, not *less* than personal," and "manifests the kind of other-directed action in creation that, in the human context, one would call love." Let us consider the assertion that UR possesses some type of "personalist" characteristics.

I acknowledge that I may be over-interpreting the authors' use of the word "personal." Lacking a background in philosophy or theology, I cannot immediately draw on knowledge of the history of the use of "person" and "personal" in Western theological thought, and so I had to do some background reading to see if I could discover why I react negatively to the use of such language to characterize the UR. I had a vague memory of hearing or reading somewhere that there had been debates among Medieval scholastics about the precise meaning of the word "person" in the context of Trinitarian deliberations.

Upon consulting various sources and general discussions of "person" in Western Medieval theological discourse, I found that the root word was employed in the ancient Greek theater to describe the masks that actors used to portray different character types. Thus the original meaning of the word might be more clearly communicated to contemporary English readers by the word *persona,* which denotes the idea that we can consciously put on and off different types of "presentations of self." Thus actors could "put on and off" different personalities.

Further reading revealed that in the Trinitarian and Christological debates of the fourth and fifth centuries, this term was used in Christian theological discourse as a part of efforts to define how the Christian deity could be both one and three. In other sources, it was noted that in contemporary analytic philosophy there is concern about a person's nature, identity, and consciousness.

Based on this review of the how "person" has been employed in Western theological discourse, it seems that originally the term was used in conjunction with other Greek ideas to provide the framework for defining the essential characteristics of the Christian deity, following the First Council of Nicaea (AD 325) and First Council of Constantinople (AD 381). Henceforth, the word was used in a Christian formula to enable a monotheist to simultaneously accept the Trinity. Such ancient wordplay should have alerted CK to the conceptual problems involved in use of "personal" to characterize UR.

For example, probably the least sophisticated criticism of the authors' use of "person" and "personal" as a descriptor for UR would be the charge that they are anthropomorphizing the divine. I might enthusiastically join in expressing such a concern except for the proviso that, with few exceptions, all of the major Western religious systems of which I'm aware, to greater and lesser degrees, employ this manner of explaining the nature of their central divine figure. It is only within the parts of religious systems espoused by intellectual elites that a decided effort is made to avoid use of such language.

It is precisely in conceiving of the UR as a "person," even within the most nuanced context, that the UR is trapped in a human-focused category. It might be argued that this is precisely the opposite of how the concept of UR should be conceptualized. However, I lack the appropriate theological or philosophical background and level of sophistication to suggest an alternate rendering. I am only aware that a tension has existed in the history of Christian thought as the emphasis on the UR's characteristics has swung from *immanence* to the idea of the *wholly other*. In the latter approach, I understand that the only human characteristic that can be applied to the UR is what the UR is *not*.

Perhaps it is helpful at this point to recall that CK present their views about the nature of UR within the mode of what they call *"minimally personalistic theism"* (MPT) as a "hypothesis." I offer another hypothesis to account for why the authors offered their hypothesis on this point. I suggest that use of "personal" as a UR descriptor was necessitated by the perceived need to provide a foundation on which to build a minimalist Christianity as one variety of a "minimally personalistic theism." My hypothesis is that CK, who are sophisticated scholars, were conscious of the logical necessity of maintaining, as they state, some minimal connection to the traditional Christian view of UR as represented in some attenuated degree by the "person" of the Jesus of history. If they would have "depersonalized" their view of UR, they may have been concerned that this would have been too widely viewed as moving their position outside of what might be called even a minimalist Christianity. In making such a statement, it should go without saying that my hypothesis on this point in no way addresses or even infers the personal commitments of the authors to their religious heritages.

"Religion" is a Modernist Construction

My final concern should probably have been inserted as a footnote. It may be dismissed as a petty focus on an obscure and irrelevant point. I would not object to such a dismissal and a banishment of it to an editorial "cutting-room floor," but I would still like to comment on this point. It follows from the title of this chapter, "The Plurality of Religions." I searched but could not locate even a hint, brief mention, or allusion—in this chapter or in the entire volume—to the *origins* of religion per se. And surely the authors are fully aware of this issue. Perhaps they assumed that any informed reader would not need to be reminded of the fundamental assumption of the modernist tradition in the West about the category "religion."

As I understand it, religion as a conceptual category is almost entirely a product of Western Enlightenment thinking. It was one intellectualist component that was included in the set of elements that came to define a normative "modernism." For most of human existence on this planet, the vast majority of societies and cultures lacked any sense of a separate or distinguishable category in their worldview or lexicon that we might translate as "religion." There were beliefs about and rituals for nearly everything in their world. These included categories that stipulated what a member of their group could and could not eat, what category of kin you can and cannot have sexual relations with, and what unseen forces had to be placated as well as what type of individual in the group was capable of dealing with these forces. The categories that we moderns use to distinguish elements of different behaviors—political, economic, and religious—were all part of a single, undifferentiated social reality.

The only point I would raise here is that the entire framework in which we are discussing this topic is, at most, 350 years old and is being expressed within a Western cultural context. If authors are addressing some type of universal proposition about UR, would it not be helpful at least to remind readers of the nature of the framework of how the discourse is being conducted?

In conclusion, given several factors: (1) all that we self-conscious, carbon-based units have learned through scientific means about the nature of the universe, (2) the long travail of our anatomically modern human species possessing language for nearly 200,000 years, and (3) our short existence on this tiny four- or five-billion-year-old planet belonging to a ordinary star off on the edge of an average galaxy, *the most rational statement that we can make about the nature of reality is that we humans don't have the cognitive means of determining why there is anything at all, let alone the nature of "UR."*

Finally, I take specific exception to the assertion that the personalist view of the UR is in any sense superior to the four alternatives that the authors offer. Of the four alternatives that are presented, I suggest that the one that presents the least objections is the authors' fourth alternative—that there is "simply no meaningful answer to the question of what is ultimately the case or why there is anything at all" (70). Obviously, if CK accepted this alternative, it is highly likely they would not have written this book and we would not be discussing it.

---

[1] Clifford Geertz, "Religion as a Cultural System," in Geertz, *The Interpretation of Cultures: Selected Essays* (Boston: Fontana Press, 1993), 87-125.

5

WHY I BELIEVE IN THE *BODILY* RESURRECTION OF JESUS AND THINK THAT CLAYTON AND KNAPP MIGHT TOO

A Reflection on Chapter 5, "The Scandal of Particularity, Part I: The Resurrection Testimony"

David R. Larson

I affirm the bodily resurrection of Jesus because I deny substance dualism. In *The Predicament of Belief*, Philip Clayton and Steven Knapp (hereafter CK) also deny substance dualism. In the following paragraphs I suggest that they might affirm the bodily resurrection of Jesus even though they say they do not.

Everything depends upon what they mean when they depict the resurrected Jesus as a "personal but nonphysical presence" (97). If by "physical" they mean any substrate whatsoever, they can't believe in the bodily resurrection and don't. But if in their denial they mean a substrate that is *basically* like our own bodies, such that the resurrected Jesus is nothing more than a resuscitated and transformed corpse, in their rejection of the "physical" they are with the Apostle Paul and I would like to be so as well. In this second case, we all would hold that the resurrected Jesus is substrate-dependent but in a *fundamentally different* way than we are.

My best reading of CK so far is that when they describe the resurrected Jesus as "personal" they mean that he is not "a person" (41). They think instead of his identity as having been adopted by and merged with God's identity and its "not-less-than-personal" (34) character. In their account of his presence as "nonphysical," they move beyond the contrary and equally unacceptable alternatives of depicting it as either a "physically embodied individual" or a "disembodied consciousness" (129). They hold, instead, that God's Spirit is the substrate of the resurrected Jesus just as his human physical body was before his death (129). Yet this is not the whole story.

Six Levels of Christian Belief

Expositions of what Christians believe about the resurrection typically proceed in one of two ways and each has its inherent strengths and weaknesses. Those that begin with what Christians uniquely hold have the advantage of staying more closely with what only Christians affirm and the disadvantage of often not becoming completely intelligible to others. Those that begin with what almost everyone believes have the advantage of making more sense to those who are not Christians and the disadvantage of frequently not making it all the way to what Christians uniquely hold. Christians and the wider public need both approaches; nevertheless, we should keep in mind their differences so as not to expect the wrong thing from either.

This book is distinctive among those that begin with wider considerations because it provides a six-level "typology of degrees of rational justification" (111-117). At level 1 the believer's convictions are those that the Relevant Community of Experts (RCE) either does or could affirm. At level 2 these convictions might not be affirmed by the RCE; however, they would be if the believer could explain to its satisfaction why the RCE is mistaken in not agreeing. In principle, then, consensus between the believer and the RCE is possible at level 1 and level 2.

This is not the case for levels 3 through 6. Beliefs at these levels are "irreducibly controversial" (113-16), albeit for different reasons and in varying degrees. At level 3 beliefs can be justifiable even though they are not affirmed by the RCE because they appropriately flow from certain "assumptions," "points of view," or "experiences" (114) on the part of the believer that members of the RCE understandably do not share. At level 4, the believer himself or herself experiences enough uncertainty and vacillation about what can be inferred from such personal considerations that belief cannot be rationally justified but only permitted. At level 5 even such rational permission is so largely unavailable that one falls short of actually believing in favor of hoping that in the end at least some of one's beliefs will turn out to be true. CK describe this level as "hope-plus-faith" (116). At level 6, for all practical purposes one has no such hope; however, in personal and liturgical events one might use the words of some religious community as metaphors that point toward rationally justified beliefs, providing that one keeps in mind that these are figures of speech which are not literally true.

To my way of thinking, this six-level typology is exceedingly helpful because it invites one to consider not only what one believes but also the types and degrees of rational justification one's beliefs may possess. This makes the difference between belief and unbelief less like an electrical on-off switch and more like a rheostat that one can set at a certain level and leave or turn up or down as changing circumstances may require. This way of construing belief is truer to the ways people actually live.

Various Interpretations of Jesus' Resurrection

CK position all the understandings of the resurrection that they offer at level 3 through level 6. Like many claims of specific religious communities that depend upon distinctive histories and insights, they are irreducibly controversial. According to the *symbolic* understanding, Jesus "was a kind of religious genius, someone whose spiritual perspicacity, imagination, and immersion in the traditions of Jewish monotheism enabled him to grasp more clearly and state more powerfully than his predecessors the universal truths that were already implicit in those traditions" (85). In my words, Jesus is "alive" today in the sense that right down to our time many experience much of what and how he taught as positive contributions.

In the *exemplary* interpretation, "Jesus was 'resurrected' only in the metaphorical sense that he provided a moral and spiritual model that would inspire and influence subsequent generations of his followers" (85). Again, in my words, it is one thing to say that Jesus was a great teacher and another to claim that he admirably lived what he taught and that we would do well to do so also. This way of understanding the resurrection of Jesus looks upon him as someone to emulate.

The *participatory* account holds that "the disciples, after Jesus' death, found themselves participating in a new reality in which their relationship with the UR [Ultimate Reality or God] had been transformed by the divine grace and freedom they had encountered in the teachings, the acts, and indeed the personal presence of Jesus" (87). Unlike the first two options, this third one suggests that in the resurrection of Jesus God actually did something that contributed to the "new reality," although what God did was in harmony with their non-interventionist understanding of divine action. According to this interpretation, the resurrection of Jesus was the actual interaction (85-7) of God and the first followers of Jesus.

The participatory view depends upon a difference CK discern in the writings of the Apostle Paul between thinking "of the individual man Jesus as literally continuing to exist" (89), on the one hand, and conceiving "of the risen Christ not so much as an individual person but as the continuation (and availability to believers) of that person's life-giving righteousness—that is, of the life-giving righteousness that Jesus had manifested during his life" (89).

Noting how "freely Paul interchanges the terms 'Spirit,' 'Spirit of God,' 'Spirit of Christ,' and 'Christ'" (87-89), they suggest that we take these expressions seriously. This does not mean that "Jesus as conscious agent possesses our minds, but that we give ourselves to God by participating in Jesus' self-surrendering obedience to God" (90).

According to what we might call the *"cosmic"* version of the participatory interpretation, the death and resurrection of Jesus took place in "boundary events," akin to the dramatic beginning and end of the universe, in which the normal patterns of regularity that we often call "laws of nature" yielded to the immense pressures of clashing overlapping cosmic epochs (97). Describing it as an attempt to clarify a mystery with an even greater mystery, CK expound this possibility but move on without endorsing it.

The *pneumatological* version of the participatory interpretation, which CK favor, contends that the resurrected Jesus himself became available to his disciples, and presumably to us, as a "nonphysical but personal presence" (109). CK distinguish this approach "both from a theory of bodily or physical presence and from the participatory theory" as such (100). According to this proposal, the "nonphysical form" (100) of the resurrected Jesus made it possible for people to encounter nothing less than his actual presence and to do so without requiring miraculous divine interventions.

CK speculate about how those who experienced the personal but nonphysical presence of the risen Jesus frequently mistook it to be physical. They suggest that in one way or another, depending upon which theory one chooses, the disciples experientially merged the two (99). For instance, perhaps their grief was so profound, their encounters with his nonphysical presence were so vivid, their memories of his physical life were so intense, their apocalyptic anticipations of a resurrection of the dead were so much at hand and, presumably, their worldviews were so unscientific, that it is understandable that they experienced him as physically present even though this was not literally so (99).

The *unsurpassable* version of the life, teachings, death, and resurrection of Jesus is about as far in the direction of Christian uniqueness that one can go. "Jesus himself, on this account, becomes not only an important instance of human participation in the divine reality but the highest, fullest, most authoritative, or most perfect instance" (95). Although CK don't dismiss this possibility out of hand, they note how difficult it is to confirm or disconfirm it. "What if," they ask, "a relatively unknown saint once lived in a small village, a person who was uniquely open to the lure of God? What if her brief life demonstrated a fusion with the divine will that matched or even exceeded Jesus' model of self-giving?" (122).

CK have little confidence in the *resuscitation* option, even though they do not always use this word. The resuscitation option is "the traditional belief that, after his death on the cross, Jesus' body was miraculously restored to life in a newly powerful and immortal form, left his tomb, and appeared to his disciples" (126). For CK, perhaps the worst feature of this traditional interpretation is that it appeals to the "miraculous." Because they understand "miracles" to be divine interventions into what we call the "laws of nature," by definition this option must be rejected in favor of their non-interventionist understanding of divine action (15).

The Complicated Nature of the Post-Easter Jesus

I hazard that the thinking of CK about the resurrection of Jesus is much more complex than resuscitation. It is true that they repeatedly and at length insist upon a "personal but nonphysical" presence. It is also the case that they reject the idea of a bodily resurrection partly because they think of it as a violation of their non-interventionist account of divine action (52-87). They hold that the bodily "ascension" of Jesus after the resurrection is "unavailable" to us (96). In addition, they speak in at least two ways about the dispensability of our physical bodies. On the one hand, looking backward, we can view this as a necessity for the eventual emergence of finite persons (38). On the other hand, looking forward, we can at least imagine and perhaps hope for a radically different set of circumstances—perhaps a different cosmological epoch—in which consciousness need not be so physically dependent (130). Yet in the end it seems to me that their most fundamental objection to the idea of the bodily resurrection of Jesus is that it violates the best forms of contemporary science (15). "What [inadmissible, in their view] miracle could be harder to accept," they ask, "than one involving the restoration to life and consciousness of a human body three days after its blood has ceased to circulate?" (15).

Despite all this compelling evidence, there are other points in their discussion at which CK seem like sailors who tack in a different direction in the face of powerful theological winds. To begin with, it is unarguably clear that they favor some form of emergence theory to substance dualism or even property dualism (28-39). It is also abundantly clear that they prefer not to think of the resurrected

Jesus as "disembodied consciousness" (129). It must also be said that they cite the Apostle Paul's reference to a "spiritual body," which either does or does not support the idea of a bodily resurrection depending upon which of these two words one emphasizes (131). And beyond CK's allusion to the idea of the bodily resurrection (Jesus circulates blood the same way we do), they describe the resurrected Jesus as "transformed" (84), "glorified and immortal" (91), "powerful and immortal" (126).

Although I probably make more of it than I should, with a different shade of meaning CK say that the resurrected Jesus *embodies* "self-surrender" (41), *embodies* "infinite grace and compassion" (104), *embodies* "self-giving love" (105), and *embodies* "self-giving love and compassion" (109). At the very least, this shows that it is more difficult to avoid the language of "embodiment" than we might first think. I think their use of this term in this setting tells us more than this. Psychiatrists would probably propose that it tells us much more.

I have a similar reaction to how CK explain how we might understand what it is that "sustains" the resurrected Jesus, an issue that emerges only if we think that it needs to be sustained by or grounded in something. Their answer is not that the personhood of the resurrected Jesus needs no "sustaining" but that it is directly sustained by the Spirit of God. In the resurrection the Spirit of God is to Jesus what his physical body previously was (110).

Although they hold that this "completes and perfects" instead of contradicting or violating what is already the case for every finite person (130), I experience some tension between thinking that the personhood of Jesus is sustained by God on the one hand, and thinking that it is adopted by and merged with God on the other. CK evidently do not feel this tension and for now I am willing to leave it at that.

Ten Observations

(1) My first reaction is that in the long run theoretical differences matter. If on my compass I am five degrees away from the route I planned for crossing the street to my friend's house, I will get there with no difficulty. If while flying from Los Angeles to Sydney, Australia I am off course by only that much, I will be in trouble.

So it is with ideas. In the short run, the ideas we choose perhaps make little difference, but over the span of a life they might, and through the centuries of a civilization they do.

(2) Although it might be the best we can do, appealing to the Relevant Community of Experts (111-127) suffers from being very contextual. Consider the following settings in one man's life, each of which has its own somewhat distinct Relevant Community of Experts: (a) the non-religious home in which he was reared; (b) the Christian college at which he first encountered the world of philosophy; (c) the evangelical seminary where he took some courses for those preparing to become Christian clergy; (d) the now secular Ivy League University where he earned doctorates in two specialties; (e) the German universities where he did his post-doctoral studies; (f) the state university at which he taught for several years; (g) the multi-religious campus where he now serves as a professor; (h) the scientific groups with which he interacts; and (i) the liberal churches he is helping to revive. He could ask the same question (does God exist?) in these various settings and get somewhat different answers because the recognized Relevant Community of Experts is quite diverse. Is there nothing more objective?

(3) I add three considerations to the two primary factors that persuade CK to insist upon a worldview that excludes divine interventions, for a total of five. One point they develop at length is that for anything good or bad to happen the life of the universe must

unfold in harmony with the predictable patterns of regularity that we call "laws of nature" to which there are no exceptions, except perhaps in "boundary events" (48). A second point they offer is that if God intervenes to forestall or remedy some great horror, on pain of being capricious, God must do so in all such cases and this would unravel the natural order (49-52). A third is that such interventions would overly tempt us to look for God in the extraordinary events of life instead of in the ordinary ones to which we should attend if we want to live balanced and healthy lives. A fourth factor is that expecting God to intervene in order to meet our needs would lead us over time toward becoming slothful and witless buffoons. A fifth is that divine interventions would rob us of the awe and wonder we often experience when we pay attention to how things in the natural world actually work.

(4) Yet excluding supernatural interventions might make less of a difference on Jesus' resurrection than we think. CK seem to reason as follows: (a) supernatural interventions never occur; (b) by definition bodily resurrections are supernatural interventions; (c) therefore, bodily resurrections never occur.

Although I try never saying "never" so as not to be discredited by one anomaly, for all practical purposes I agree with (a). My concurrence is probabilistic rather than metaphysical, however. In other words, I prefer observing what God does or does not do to telling God what is or is not possible. This is why I do not agree with (b) and therefore do not conclude (c).

If at (b) we substituted the word "miracles" for "resurrections," would most of us agree? I think not. Although people as different as David Hume and C. S. Lewis define "miracles," at least provisionally, as "supernatural events that contradict the laws of nature," or something similar, this is not how most of us depict them.

It is more likely that we, along with many others over the centuries, depict them as "events that surpass *what we now know* about the natural world." Less frequently but more precisely, we define them as occurrences of any sort that evoke awe and wonder. This would be closer to the root meaning of the English word. Also, the New Testament speaks of "signs," "wonders," and "powers."

CK are convincing when they argue that the resurrection of Jesus was wholly natural; however, to me they are less persuasive when they assert that for this reason it could not have been bodily. This might have been the result of God working in, with, and through what we call nature's "laws."

As a human being who often flies six miles above the earth at five hundred miles an hour, frequently talks to people on the other side of the world as though they were in the same room, listens to radios and watches television, warms his food in a microwave oven, drives an automobile, saves documents on a thumb drive, and does many other similar things, all of which would have been deemed "unnatural" and therefore "impossible" for most of human history, I'm not qualified to say what is or is not possible within the laws of nature. It is possible for an event to be wholly natural even though it seems otherwise to me.

(5) I would like to see books like this one put more emphasis on objective immortality, the teaching that at the very least we all survive death as objects within God's memory. This is what most of the people in First Testament times apparently believed. This is what most fits with all the deaths we daily see around and among us. And this is what one often finds in the schools of contemporary thought that I respect the most.

Most of the time I hope for more than this at level 5 and feel justified in doing so on the basis of what CK call "the Christian proposition"

(81-5); however, there are moments when I'm at level 6 and don't. On these occasions I turn to the Apostle Paul's conviction that "neither death, nor life, nor angels, nor rulers, nor things present, nor things to come, nor powers, nor height, nor death, nor anything else in all creation will be able to separate us from the love of God in Christ Jesus our Lord" (Rom. 8:38-9). This is more than enough.

(6) I do not understand how we can develop conceptual systems that are coherent and compelling without the idea that we survive death as conscious subjects and then unfold this line of thought in a somewhat ad hoc way, because without such a system all those whose lives were horribly mangled will never experience joy (104).

To my way of thinking this terrible outcome intensifies the question without providing an answer. Maybe a loving God would want all those who suffered greatly in this life to have another opportunity for happiness; however, maybe for reasons that we do not understand, such a God wouldn't. My hesitancy at this point goes along with my preference for observing rather than instructing God at work. Discussions of the likelihood of conscious life after death ought to be based on the best evidence and reasoning, without what we think God should do to alter the outcome.

(7) We should not think that the idea of a bodily resurrection is more challenging for us than it was for people in ancient times because we are scientific and they weren't. The Babylonians, Persians, Egyptians, Greeks, and Romans were more informed about the natural world and its regularities than many of us think. In any case, their civilizations would not have had to be very "scientific" for them to know that resurrections do not occur. What's more, a number of those with whom the Apostle Paul interacted did not even want to be resurrected. For them this prospect was implausible; more than that, it was disgusting.

Notice where in this story some philosophers in Athens lost interest in Paul's message and turned to other things, some politely and others not: "When they heard of the resurrection of the dead, some scoffed; but others said, 'We will hear you again about this'" (Acts 17:32). Many today would like to believe in the resurrection of the body but cannot do so with intellectual integrity; however, for many of the ancients the very thought of it was appalling.

(8) CK's overall argument would have been more persuasive to me if, in harmony with the Relevant Community of Experts, they had outlined the differences among resuscitations, restorations, and resurrections. The biblical story of the prophet who stretched his warm body over an unresponsive boy and pushed air from his lungs into the lad's with excellent results is an example of the first. The return of Lazarus to life at the call of Jesus is illustrative of the second. And what happened in the case of the resurrection of Jesus is an instance of the third.

Some take these stories as historically factual and others don't, but the point is the same either way. It is that the decisive difference between resuscitations and restorations, on one hand, and resurrections, on the other, is that the first two are "returns" whereas the second is a "change." This change is not cosmetic but basic.

(9) In his correspondence with the first Christians at Corinth, the Apostle Paul contends that, even though we do not call it "resurrection," people who are alive can experience this thoroughgoing change as well. "Listen," he writes, "I will tell you a mystery. We will not all die, but we will all be changed, in a moment, in the twinkling of an eye, at the last trumpet" (1 Cor. 15:51). Contrary to what many suppose but in harmony with what the Apostle Paul wrote, *one need not be dead in order to experience this change.* Resurrection is neither resuscitation nor restoration but thorough transformation.

No one in the New Testament spends more time talking about this transformation than the Apostle Paul. Against those who were a bit like the reductionist materialists of our time, he made a case for the resurrection, first in Jesus and then for others. And against people who were a little like today's substance dualists, he contended that resurrection life is embodied.

Paul distinguishes different kinds of "flesh" (humans, animals, birds, fish), different kinds of "bodies" (heavenly and earthly), and different kinds of "glories" (sun, moon, and stars). In each of these clusters he emphasizes lasting similarities and differences (1 Cor. 15:39-41).

When he turns to agricultural analogies, Paul highlights transformations: "So it is with the resurrection of the dead. What is sown is perishable, what is raised is imperishable. It is sown in dishonor, it is raised in glory. It is sown in weakness, it is raised in power. It is sown a physical life, it is raised a spiritual body. If there is a physical body, there is also a spiritual body" (1 Cor. 15:42-44).

Given the conceptual resources of his time and place, it would have been easy for Paul to have depicted resurrection existence as either the restoration of life to a corpse or the emancipation of an immortal soul. Instead, he intentionally described it as a "spiritual body," and this is fundamentally different from both.

Without pretending to know what they meant to those who wrote them, I interpret the stories of the resurrected Jesus passing through doors, walking on water, walking with two men and then disappearing from their meal together, and the like, as saying in narrative form something similar to what Paul says discursively. This is that in some ways the resurrected Jesus is like us but in other ways he is fundamentally different.

(10) I suggest that CK make a constructive contribution precisely at this point. Given the way they frequently contrast the "physical" and the "personal" at important junctures throughout their book, it is tempting to think that when all is said and done they turn out to be substance dualists after all. Although I'm not absolutely certain, I think that it would be a mistake to yield to this temptation.

A more likely possibility is that, in their announced integration of emergence theory and the participatory theory of the resurrected Jesus, for them what the Apostle Paul calls the "mind of Christ" is so far advanced that it is substrate-independent or entirely bodiless or without a physical character of any sort. This alternative would not be substance dualism but a hyper-emergence account and for this reason it might be closer to their views. Yet in this discussion the consequences would be similar to the message of substance dualism: being bodily is dispensable.

Again, although I am not absolutely certain, I think that a third possibility is the best reckoning of what they mean. This is that for them in the resurrected Jesus the "mind of Christ" does depend upon a substrate; however, because of the thoroughgoing transformation that the Apostle Paul describes, this physical or bodily substrate is no longer a human body but the Spirit of God (129-30). As I indicated at the outset, this is about as good an account of the bodily resurrection of Jesus as we can get or should desire.

This suggestion will be jarring to those for whom God's Spirit is entirely bodiless. My suggestion will make more sense if one takes it that God's Spirit is not the third member of the Trinity but God as such with a di-polar nature: mental and physical, primordial and consequent. The suggestion might also be more intelligible if one is a panentheist of some sort who agrees with the Apostle Paul and the Greek poets he quotes that God is the One "in whom we live and move and have our being" (Acts 17:27-8). Given these premises, the radical transformation of which the Apostle Paul speaks is not heterograft transplantation.

Here is the bottom line: if CK hold that the "mind of Christ" is substrate dependent in this *thoroughly* transformed way, I suggest that they believe in the bodily resurrection of Jesus. But if they think the "mind of Christ" is completely substrate-independent, they do not.

Substrate-dependence or substrate-independence? This is the question!

Substrate-Dependence or Substrate-Independence?

Isn't this a very fine line? Yes. Doesn't this make pondering it a waste of time? No. Why not? The answer is that the difference between substrate-dependence and substrate-independence are different points on our conceptual compass that might matter only a little in the short run but much in the long run. What, then, is the issue? How we view and treat our physical bodies.

Plato thought of the body as a prison. Paul thought of it as a temple and ever since many have tried to think of it as both, without success. The result is a love-hate relationship with the body and everything material in personal and cultural life, the sort of thing we see crudely in the "Madonna-whore complex."

Substance dualism, specifically the type that we have inherited from René Descartes, the so-called father of modern philosophy, strikes me as an exceedingly refined version of the same dynamic. We have extended substance ("matter") and we have thinking substance ("mind") and they are so fundamentally different that ever since the seventeenth century we have been trying to figure out what to do with them.

Achieving conceptual coherence has been and continues to be a challenge. We have dualists, we have idealists, we have materialists, we have occasionalists, we have parallelists, and we have interactionists, and after several centuries we still have perplexities. This should tell us something.

Perhaps most seriously, when we fundamentally divide mind and matter, over time we usually intensify our appreciation of the first and our depreciation of the second. The result is a culture-wide ambivalence about the physical dimensions of life: physical labor, sex, money, non-human animals, the fragile ecological order, and so forth.

In my view the most subtle and serious dynamic, which might be a cause of substance dualism and its siblings as much as a result, is a widespread restlessness and impatience with being the finite and physical creatures we are. I experience this most keenly when reading about different cosmological epochs in which we might escape our physical identities with substrate-independent consciousnesses (130).

The more I hear or read about such possibilities, the more I summon the doctrine of objective immortality. It literally keeps us grounded.

6

NON-REDUCTIVE PHYSICALISM VERSUS THE SPECTOR OF CLASSICAL DUALISM

A Reflection on Chapter 6, "The Scandal of Particularity, Part II: Jesus and the Ultimate Reality"

Calvin Thomsen

I must begin with a few words about the influence Philip Clayton has had on my life. I first heard him speak at a philosophy of religion conference a few years ago and knew at once that I was in the presence of a truly exciting thinker. His ability to interface science with theology and philosophy, his interdisciplinary perspective, his theological depth, and the clear and compelling way he put his thoughts into words made a vivid impression. My appreciation is not limited to the intellectual arena. Philip's animating passion separates him from a host of dry academics. I find both heart and urgency in the way he approaches the formidable challenges to Christian belief, and in his commitment to making ideas relevant to ministry and mission.

In this collaborative volume with Steven Knapp we find synthesis and a more fully developed integration of many of the ideas that he has written about before, and a direct attempt to address the many challenges that threaten traditional Christian theism. *The Predicament of Belief* covers many basic issues: science and religion, evil and suffering, Christianity vis-à-vis other world religions, preservation and transmission of Scripture, and the unique resurrection of Christ.

Clayton and Knapp (hereafter CK) strongly assert that it is possible to take these issues seriously without abandoning Christian claims or becoming agnostic. They believe that engaging Christian claims is profoundly important, and this differentiates them from Christian agnostics in two ways. First, they refuse to decide in advance that there is no way to assess the validity of Christian claims. Nor are they willing to give up on the importance of the quest. It is, in fact, "not just an intellectual game but an urgent religious responsibility" (19).

This book also presents a courageous willingness to face the challenges directly and not retreat into a world of what the authors call "immunization." They use this term to refer to any sort of escapism that puts Christian claims in a safe zone protected from all criticism, internal or external. "For those who reject such strategies and yet still want to know whether the Christian understanding of ultimate reality is viable," assert CK, "there is only one alternative, and that is to understand the reasons for doubt as fully and clearly as possible: to look those reasons, so to speak, directly in the eye" (14).

Resurrection as Participation in the Ultimate Reality

Chapter 6 is the second chapter that focuses on the particularity of the resurrection of Christ. The key organizing principle in this chapter is the development of what CK refer to as the "participatory theory." This theory affirms that what is present both to the original disciples after the crucifixion and to countless followers of Christ isn't the literal, physical Jesus but a relationship to a "divine reality in which Jesus' followers find themselves able to participate. What they encounter is the Spirit of Christ, who calls them to the same kenotic or self-giving love that Jesus embodied and enacted in his relationship with the one he called 'Father'" (105).

Their view of the nature and origins of Jesus could be seen as a form of "adoptionism" (a term they themselves use). They do not believe that Jesus started as a preexisting member of the Trinity who became incarnate and then returned to his heavenly state. He started as a human and his life-changing significance was acquired, rather than being a preexisting ontological reality. In describing his acquired role they offer an alternative to two polarities: "By using the traditional language of 'mutual indwelling' and 'co-mingling,' we implicitly deny the dichotomy that *either* Jesus continues as the identical person within the Godhead *or* Jesus is a merely human model for others to emulate" (103, CK's emphases).

They do affirm a type of resurrection but it does not mean that Jesus in a physical body marched triumphantly from the tomb and mingled with his disciples for forty days before ascending, also with a literal/physical body, to some place called heaven. Nor does it mean that Jesus is "personally" present with them in the weeks that followed Holy Week. He was not "present to his first disciples after his death as a personal agent, a center of subjectivity with human memories, thoughts, and wishes" (104). Rather, the disciples have a new kind of participatory relationship with the divine reality. This is experienced in the form of an encounter with "the Spirit of Christ, who calls them to the same kenotic or self-giving love that Jesus embodied and enacted in his relationship with the one he called 'Father'" (105). CK are arguing for something more than what neurologists would call an internalized sense of the other, some kind of mass hallucination, or a purely mystical experience involving a ghost or apparition.

In their view, Jesus became the most powerful link between human beings and God. This is not because of his preexisting identity or expanded human capabilities but because of something powerful that God does through him and because of him. In their words, "it isn't that Jesus suddenly becomes capable of looking through the infinite eyes of God, but that God chooses to look through the finite eyes of Jesus. We see God through Jesus' self-giving love, and God sees us through Jesus' self-giving obedience. *Together, these movements of love for the other on the part of both creator and creature constitute the self-emptying or kenotic 'mind of Christ,'* and that new reality becomes at the same time the Spirit of Christ in which both humanity and God participate" (108-9, CK's emphasis).

Because of Jesus something life-changing happened in the lives of his followers that gave them a new relationship with the divine reality. The love, service, God-connection, and perspectives of Christ became part of their lives; the ongoing Spirit of Christ dwelt in their lives.

Critique

The participatory model presented in this chapter is a vivid reminder that there are ways to build robust and passionately engaged faith without avoiding the tough questions. New ways of understanding Jesus can actually fuel a passion for living out the principles of his life. I appreciate the honesty the authors bring to the quest and the effort to develop a synthesis that actually addresses the predicaments that face believing Christians. I think it's a worthy attempt to solve some particularly vexing problems by formulating an approach to belief that doesn't blunt the challenges or give in to any form of immunizing intellectual escapes.

I have some concerns as well. At times I find myself clearer about what the authors have jettisoned than about the actual meaning of the alternative they describe. If I had been a "participating" disciple in the weeks following Calvary, what would I have experienced? What would I have seen or heard? As part of a gathered company of participating disciples, would we all have experienced something similar at the same time and place? How would I know the nature of the link between my participation and the Jesus with whom I had walked the roads of Palestine, fished from the Sea of Galilee, and engaged in earnest conversation over the breaking of bread? How would I experience the call of Jesus to kenotic or self-giving love? The limitation of understanding may be my own, and the meaning of the participatory language may be clearer to others than it is to me.

There are two issues I will address in more detail: the first is CK's application of the "not even once" principle to Jesus' resurrection, and the second is the role of physicality in our understanding of Jesus, science, and philosophy/theology.

Not Even Once

CK offer a detailed description of a "not even once" principle in Chapter 3. God "lacks the luxury of human finitude" (51). Therefore God cannot intervene in some cases of human suffering while failing to intervene in others. If God did this "even once," it would create a chain reaction of moral obligation to do the same in countless other cases of innocent human suffering. This would be true of both overt interventions and more subtle/hidden interventions. In addition to what seems like a moral justice component, CK are also saying that the sort of world that develops rational, moral, and autonomous agents requires a world characterized by regularity, one in which natural laws can be trusted.

CK don't present a picture devoid of hope, and this hope exists because they don't extend their non-intervention principle to all places and times. They affirm that "the grace and compassion of God can only be defended adequately if it makes sense to suppose that there is hope for a continuation of human existence beyond the grave. Otherwise, the unmerited suffering and despair that have defined the lives of so many human beings over so many millennia seem to be not only pointless but unredeemed and unredeemable" (104). They further affirm that Jesus "shares the eschatological future available to other human beings" (104). Thus, Jesus provides the foundation for hope beyond death.

In the face of vast oceans of human suffering, the "not even once" principle would create a kind of logical consistency. In that one regard, it parallels Calvinism. Calvinism creates consistency by proclaiming that everything, including all of what we consider evil, is part of God's perfect plan. There is a single unifying principle behind both good and evil—everything that happens is a result of the direction of a sovereign God.

CK approach the same problem from the opposite direction by asserting that nothing that happens in this world is under the direct control of God. It is only God's will in that God has arranged the world a certain way—a way that allows for creaturely freedom and provides the people a growing dynamic of emergent complexity. Since God has not created a world in which the divine hand arrests the collapse of a building in an earthquake, stops the murder of a missionary, or shields a child from sexual violation at the hands of a predator, God is, in fact, consistent in divine non-intervention. God does not capriciously swoop in to unearth the missing car keys from under the sofa cushions for a frantically praying believer who is late to work while demurely standing back and doing nothing as a tsunami washes over a village, killing its inhabitants. There is a way in which this principle affirms both the moral consistency of God and God's commitment to a particular type of predictable world that allows both scientific knowledge and personal development.

It is not totally clear to me, however, how moving divine intervention to some realm beyond the grave solves the "not even once" challenge. If God can accomplish this at all, in any place and time, I'm not sure that this relocation solves the basic philosophical problem of intervention.

But let us assume that it is at least logically possible that there could be some type of "eternity exemption" that allows God to intervene to put an end to suffering in the next world without obligating him to use that same capacity on our behalf now. If this were the case, does the logic of "not even once" preclude some type of dramatic revelatory activity in which the future breaks into the present in the person and work of Jesus?

The carefully reasoned arguments in Chapter 3 hinge largely on the issue of God's intervention to relieve human suffering and the need for a world that develops free moral beings in a predictable world. But it could be argued that Jesus did not intervene in human life for the purpose of offering random relief from suffering. He talks about setting the captives free, but he doesn't literally free slaves. He has much to say about justice, but he doesn't overthrow Roman oppression. He is gravely concerned about economic injustice and poverty, but he doesn't rain down shekels and denarii upon the poor. Even if we did view miracles such as healing in a more traditional sense (and I'm not saying that we must), they are never presented as random and fortunate health care treatments or even as a way of increasing the odds that followers of Christ will live long and healthy lives. In fact many of them had their lives abruptly cut short—often as a direct result of their commitment as followers of Christ.

I would suggest that there might be a distinction between "intervention" and "revelation." My argument, while not about miracles in general, follows reasoning similar to that of David Allan Hubbard who states that "the primary motive for divine miracle is not compassion but revelation."[1] I would use the term "intervention" to refer to ways in which God might alter the normal progression of events to relieve human suffering and improve the quality of life on earth. Revelation, even if it sometimes involves similar activities, is defined by a different purpose—that of providing a defining glimpse of an eschatological future in ways that meaningfully shape and define the sorts of lives we are to live now in anticipation of its ultimate realization when things shall be "on earth as they are in heaven."[2]

The death and resurrection of Christ is presented as unique, something that happened once and only once. In this sense it is different from miracles, divine providence, or any other activity of God. It is "once for all" (Rom. 6:10; Heb. 7:25, 9:16) and the "first fruits" (1 Cor. 15:20) of the ultimate eschatological destiny possible for human beings. Theologians often define it as "the presence of the future," or the proleptic experience of the eschaton breaking into human life as we know it (for example, see Ladd, *Presence of the Future*).[3]

If in this act of revelation Jesus didn't even grant his closest followers a life of reduced suffering, it's hard to see how anything in his life, death, and resurrection would incur an obligation to globally reduce or eliminate all suffering for everybody else on this side of the eschaton.

It also seems possible that the singular, unique events of the life, death, and resurrection of Jesus could do much to foster the kind of human development CK describe in Chapter 3. This glimpse of the eschatological future could define the divine mission and inspire the followers of Christ to overturn slavery, fight for social justice, improve the economic state of the poor, and engage in acts that promote healing and wholeness.

The Issue of Physicality

The most significant challenge I would raise concerns the issue of physicality and its relationship to the spiritual. In several ways this chapter seems to be suggesting that removing or at least diminishing the physicality of certain aspects of Jesus, particularly in the time following the events of Holy Week, creates a paradigm more compatible with science and more adequate to address the difficult "predicament of belief" questions.

Religious conservatives often seem to be focused on the need to have everything very literal and physical in order for it to be meaningful. Everything about the Garden of Eden and the events described therein must be literal in ways that accord with our Western reading of them. If the author of Hebrews refers to a heavenly sanctuary of which the earthy version is a type, then the one in heaven must have literal drapes, furnishings, roof, etc. The same care for literal physicality applies to such things as Noah's ark or the great fish that swallowed Jonah.

Progressives, on the other hand, often seem to have a profound level of discomfort with this sort of physicalism. They often want to preserve the core of the Christ event or other significant points but feel that they can best do this by extracting the physicality of such events. Significant events become metaphoric, subjective internal experiences, or "spiritual" experiences without direct physical correlates.

While I understand progressives' concerns about wooden literalism, I'm not sure that I want to totally concede physicality to the literalists. The scientific enterprise is based on a high view of the physical world. It seems to me that there may in fact be certain advantages, even from a scientific point of view, in maintaining a high enough view of the physical world to embrace the possibility that Jesus could have been a physical being with conscious awareness who fellowshipped with his disciples following a resurrection event. This would also be compatible with a view that the Christian hope involves resurrected bodies. On the one hand, this view is difficult to accept. But on the other hand, it seems stronger in its affirmation of the physical world than a spiritualized view of Christ which, at least on the surface, sounds more like a paranormal experience than something compatible with modern science.

In addition to the link between physicality and science, I think there is a compelling case for an overall theological/philosophical perspective that moves us in a more holistic direction, where spiritual realities are linked more closely with the physical dimension rather than moved away from it. A holistic perspective is gaining ground in many sectors of the theological community, and is core to a point of emphasis in Seventh-day Adventist theology, where it is both a theological belief and a very practical guide with implications for medical work, promotion of physical health, and care for the world. It also has implications for one's view of death and the resurrection. In this view, eternal destiny is not found in some disembodied state but as whole, resurrected beings with physical bodies. This perspective is being given a very articulate voice by a number of theologians from various strands of Christendom who embrace "non-reductionist physicalism." The book, *Whatever Happened to the Soul?*[4] clearly articulates this model. Theologian Nancey Murphy has written extensively on the topic, while Warren Brown and Malcolm Jeeves are examples of theologically informed neuroscientists who address these issues.[5]

In this perspective, "spiritual" factors, at least as they pertain to human beings, have neurobiological correlates. This does not mean that they can be reduced to them, only that they are revealed in them and don't exist without them. In a sense, these contemporary theological writers are pulling the spiritual dimension out of the Platonic sky and back into physical bodies. We do not have a soul tethered to a physical body ready to be released at death or some other point in the future; we *are* souls. And all of our capacities, from the most physical acts such as eating to our most sublime states of spiritual awareness, are rooted in our biological existence. They are not "merely" biological states or limited to them, but are experienced within them.

Much of what CK affirm in the second part of Chapter 3 sounds very compatible with non-reductionist physicalism. But, at least from my reading of Chapter 6, there are several specific points at which they seem to be moving away from, rather than toward, a full embrace of the physical as the setting for the spiritual.

I know that there are important ways in which the undergirding philosophy of panentheism differs from classic dualism at an ontological level. It denies the existence of two separate forms of "stuff." Still, CK's notion of a "pneumatological" Christ who was spiritually real to the disciples but not actually physically "there" for them, the ways the authors depict the world beyond death, the implication (at least as I read it) that the afterlife of both Jesus and the rest of the human family does not/will not exist in the form of physically resurrected bodies, and even the reasons they give for rejecting the bodily resurrection of Jesus create a certain kind of dualistic overtone. It seems to move us closer to Plato or Descartes than to science. And, while it may solve some philosophical and scientific problems, it could create others.

I think another advantage of a non-reductive physicalist perspective is that it doesn't require a high degree of elasticity from the biblical texts concerning the resurrection. CK look for helpful links between the post-Easter texts and historical interpretations, and they don't try to bend the texts in order to put all of their own words back into the minds of the biblical writers. They aren't afraid to acknowledge some differences, and I applaud them for that.

Still, I think it is worthwhile to look at the meaning of the term "resurrection" in its Jewish context, something that many centuries of Christian theology have often obscured rather than illuminated. On the meaning of the term, I am indebted to the work of N. T. Wright. I am not commenting on his overall conclusions (or the ways he uses the background research to affirm them), but I do think that his careful and exhaustive research on the term and its historical background in books such as *The Resurrection of the Son of God*[6] and *Surprised by Hope*[7] are significant. There were all sorts of beliefs about life after death and the nature of the afterlife floating around in the world in which Jesus lived, but these views would have been described in other language. No Jew at the time of Jesus, according to Wright, would have accepted the term resurrection to refer to anything other than a literal/physical event in which bodily death was followed by bodily life. A revival of faith and meaning, a mystical experience of inner illumination, going to heaven after death, or the ongoing existence of some kind of soul or spirit being, or even Jesus becoming divine would not be described in the language of resurrection. Other terms would have been used for those options, since resurrection was a clear reference to physical bodies. Wright also strongly asserts that the reference to a "spiritual body" in 1 Corinthians 15:44, while not the same as a natural or mortal body, is most definitely not a reference to a non-physical body.

It seems to me that a more "holistic" perspective, which more comfortably embraces the physical world and isn't so quick to rule out a bodily resurrected Christ, has the potential to be friendly to science and philosophically robust with the added advantage of staying closer to the New Testament descriptions.

What speak to me most powerfully in this book are not the specific details of the solutions that CK propose. It is the case the authors make for belief and passionate commitment even when evidence doesn't "force" a conclusion. We can't simply remain on the sidelines when much is at stake for individuals and churches. There is an appeal to the heart and a call for action in this book that I find very compelling. And, for somebody like me for whom the questions are very real, they offer a hopeful and clear framework for belief and passionate commitment in the face of the unanswered questions. They make it clear that there is a subjective element to belief. And they offer, primarily in Chapter 7, a particularly clear and logical approach for interfacing the intellectual aspects and evidence with that subjective dimension. For me, the book's intellectual-affective unity emerge as the most powerful and meaningful contribution.

I found the specific models of Chapter 6 less clear and satisfying than that overall perspective. And, in keeping with their treatment of subjective factors, I can see ways in which my concerns may reflect some of my own subjective bias. My most recent field of academic training and research (social neuroscience) has given me a deepening appreciation for the neurobiological dimensions of even the most sublime, poetic, and spiritual aspects of human experience such as love and faith. Seventh-day Adventist and Loma Linda University "wholeness" perspectives also inform my thinking.

And, simply from an intellectual perspective, I have never found that substituting "spiritual" interpretations in the place of more physical models of events such as the resurrection does anything to settle any of my doubts. They make me think back to those strange times when somebody called wanting to register for the engaged couples premarital class I've run on the campus of Loma Linda University for many years. I've actually had people ask for an exception to the policy that couples attend together because the caller claims to be engaged to a very well-known celebrity who is "too busy" to attend the class. No matter how passionately they affirm that they are indeed engaged to the celebrity (who may, in reality, be married to somebody else) or how earnestly they explain that this person is the light of their life—the one with whom they experience some type of communion of souls, and the one who lives within their heart—I have one demand. I tell them that all they have to do is get their famous celebrity fiancé, in bodily form, to attend class the first night "even once," and we will work out alternative arrangements for the other sessions. Call me a hard-hearted skeptic, but I insist that the subjective experience of the beloved correlates with an actual person in an actual relationship.

Although I would have appreciated a model that didn't rely quite so heavily on the "pneumatological" Christ, I can affirm the significance of this book. While I am not always convinced by some of the arguments used, the way the authors put it all together at the end is helpful and convincing.

---

[1] David Allan Hubbard, "Foreword," in *Ministry and the Miraculous: A Case Study at Fuller Theological Seminary,* ed. Lewis Smedes (Pasadena, CA: Fuller Theological Seminary, 1987), 13.
[2] Ibid.
[3] George Eldon Ladd, *The Presence of the Future: The Eschatology of Biblical Realism* (Grand Rapids, MI: Eerdmans, 1974).
[4] Warren Brown, Nancey C. Murphy, and H. Newton Maloney, *Whatever*

Happened to the Soul? Scientific and Theological Portraits of Human Nature (Minneapolis: Fortress Press, 1998).
[5]Malcolm Jeeves and Warren S. Brown, *Neuroscience, Psychology, and Religion: Illusions, Delusions, and Realities about Human Nature* (West Conshohocken, PA: Templeton Foundation Press, 2009).
[6] N. T. Wright, *The Resurrection of the Son of God* (Minneapolis: Fortress Press, 2003).
[7] N. T. Wright, *Surprised by Hope: Rethinking Heaven, the Resurrection, and the Mission of the Church* (New York: Harper-Collins Publishers, 2008).

7
PRIVATE EVIDENCE AND RESPONSIBLE BELIEF

A Reflection on Chapter 7, "Doubt and Belief"
Richard Rice

Philip Clayton is the last, the very last, figure that Gary Dorrien discusses in his monumental three-volume history of liberal theology.[1] And what Dorrien says about Clayton in this passage bears directly on the task that he undertakes in *The Predicament of Belief*. Insisting that he is a "liberal theologian," Clayton affirms the classical liberal project of integrating the best human knowledge with the Christian tradition. And it was the liberal openness to science—in contrast to the conservative resistance to scientific conclusions that conflict with religious beliefs—that drew him into the liberal camp. While Clayton insists that he stands in the tradition of liberal theology, with its commitment to render the contents of faith intelligible to the modern mind, *The Predicament of Belief* suggests that Clayton is nevertheless resistant to the liberal tendency, as he sees it, to dismiss too quickly various traditional Christian claims which the "modern mind" finds problematic. Instead, Clayton wants to embrace more of what Christians have traditionally affirmed, a move that gives him affinities with evangelicals and open theists (which it gives me pleasure to note). For example, Clayton advocates "open panentheism," a process metaphysics that shares certain features with conservative Christianity, such as the notion of creatio ex nihilo.

Clayton's description of those who "may be minimalists in what they believe, but...maximalists in the confidence with which they believe it" brings to mind one of my professors at the University of Chicago. Schubert M. Ogden has been more or less accurately described as a left-wing Bultmannian because of his insistence that the claims of Christianity must be thoroughly demythologized in order to be accessible to the modern mind. This led him to the formulation that Jesus Christ is the decisive re-presentation of the original possibility for authentic human existence that is available to every human being by virtue of the gracious presence of God, the supreme reality in whom all things live and move and have their being. (It is thus the "Christ of faith," not the "Jesus of history," which provides the object of Christian faith and of theological concern.) And since this understanding of human being requires an affirmation of divinity, Ogden develops powerful, and—to me—thoroughly persuasive arguments for the reality of God. So, while the expanse or scope of what Christians meaningfully claim is highly compressed for a liberal theologian like Ogden, the evidence he marshals to support this core is impressive, to say the least.

Six Levels of Rationality

I mention Ogden to illustrate by contrast that this is not the solution to the predicament of belief which Clayton and colleague Steven Knapp (hereafter CK) propose. They do not resolve the tension between the universality of religious claims about ultimate reality and the historical particularity of Christianity's claims about Jesus by diminishing or dismissing the latter. Instead, CK propose a highly nuanced view of the way, or ways, in which believers—those who find the claims of traditional Christianity problematic from the standpoint of responsible scientific and historical investigation, and yet attractive, if not irresistible, from a personal standpoint—can frankly address their doubts without losing their faith. The central purpose of Chapter 7 is to show that there are degrees or levels of rationality and not a single standard of rationality (111). Accordingly, CK provide what they variously refer to as an epistemic scale (128), a typology of degrees of rational justification (115-16), and "a sufficiently nuanced framework for assessing the rational status of belief" (118).

CK offer no fewer than six different levels or degrees of justification (115-17), depending on the relative strength of the evidence in favor of a belief (and "belief-like" attitudes [118]), and correspondingly it seems, the relative confidence of the believer in the truth of her belief. Accordingly, a belief that fails to satisfy one level of rationality, and is not fully justified, may nevertheless prove to be rational by other criteria. Moreover, there are multiple ways in which a rational agent can be committed to any particular religious claim (134):

> (1) *Scientific beliefs*. S believes P and believes that P is endorsed by the relevant community of experts (RCE). To paraphrase this situation, a believer affirms a proposition because she finds the public evidence for it to be conclusive.
>
> (2) *Minimally personalistic theism (implications of level 1 claims)*. S believes P even though the RCE does not because she believes the RCE is mistaken in rejecting it and she has a "theory of error" that explains that rejection. In this case the believer affirms the proposition because it enjoys conclusive public evidence, even

though the strength of that evidence is not fully appreciated. (It should be public, but the relevant public does not yet appreciate it.)

(3) *Concrete and controversial claims of religious traditions (by participants)*. S believes P even though she does not expect the RCE ever to accept it, because her personal experiences nevertheless make it reasonable for her to believe. Though the belief may lack conclusive public evidence, her own experience provides sufficient (private) evidence to justify it. Accordingly, the belief will remain irreducibly controversial, because it lacks—and apparently will always lack—conclusive public evidence. Nevertheless, the RCE will acknowledge that she is justified in holding that belief, even though it does not find sufficient evidence to support it (cf. distinction between valid and sound arguments in elementary logic).

(4) *Claims that RCE would not recognize, even as valid for the subject*. This is a very difficult level to describe or evaluate. S believes P even though she does not expect the RCE ever to accept it, and unlike (3), she does not expect the RCE to regard her own reasons as good ones. Indeed, she herself is not sure that her personal experience provides enough evidence to justify the belief. Nevertheless, she finds sufficient private evidence to render the belief rationally permissible.

(5) *Religious hopes*. S no longer believes P. She no longer has good reasons for doing so, but she *hopes* that it will turn out to be true. Someone in this situation is no longer a "believer," but is more accurately described as a "seeker." In other aspects of the religious life—when it comes to worship, decision-making, or an understanding of one's identity, for example—the seeker may be identical to the believer. The posture of hope provides a kind of "cognitive policy" that falls short of actual belief.

(6) *Metaphorical Religion.* S no longer believes P, nor has any hope that P will turn out to be true. But she finds in P a valuable metaphor for a proposition or propositions that she believes are true. She may even suspend her disbelief while participating in communal worship and other shared experiences with believers. And she may have occasional moments of conviction.[2]

CK are convinced that having good reasons for one's beliefs, and for knowing just what level of justification applies to one's beliefs, is important. As they rightly insist, our most important decisions should be based on reasons that we think are good ones (118). We cannot abdicate our intellectual responsibilities. We must look for reasons to support our beliefs, and we should realistically and humbly assess the strength of these reasons. If they are weak, let's admit it.

First of all, I appreciate the fundamental concern of this book. No question is more basic than the reliability of our beliefs—in any area, and particularly in the area of religion. The nature of knowledge has always been an essential part of philosophy. And in modern philosophy it has become the most important question of all. According to influential thinkers such as René Descartes and Immanuel Kant, we don't have the right to claim that something is true unless we can adequately account for the way we came to know or believe it. So, the question is not just what do we know, but how do we know that we know?

I also appreciate CK's attempt to portray the complexities that characterize (or afflict!) believers who seek to be intellectually responsible, to provide evidence for their beliefs, as well as remaining faithful to their convictions. I appreciate even more, perhaps, the various ways in which they acknowledge the difficulty and subtlety of this endeavor.

The Equivalent Value of Public and Private Evidence

CK acknowledge the important difference between what I like to call public and private evidence. There is evidence that is available to any informed, reasonable person, and there is evidence that is accessible only to an individual herself. Often, the stronger evidence is of the latter sort. People often make important decisions on the basis of private rather than public evidence. Having private evidence, therefore, is not the same as having no evidence at all. The question is not whether there is evidence or not, but whether the most important evidence bearing on a decision is available to any objective, disinterested observer.[3]

Here and there throughout the chapter CK interject comments that significantly qualify the enterprise they carefully outline. First of all, there is no way to step outside one's beliefs to compare them to reality itself (112). Second, no matter how nuanced the standard of justification may be, it is extremely difficult to assess the rationality of one's beliefs. For one thing, human beings are not entirely, or even largely, rational in their approach to their own beliefs. Some care about such things more than others. Even those who want good reasons for their beliefs will rely on some beliefs they can't rationally justify, and no one can cite a rational basis for every belief she holds (111). And it is particularly difficult to assess such a personal and urgent matter as one's own religious belief (118). In addition, a person is likely to slide up and down the scale of rationality in the course of her religious experience (120). And it is quite possible that someone will "adhere more strongly" to a belief that has less justification, or is even irrational by her own standards, than to one that has more (120).

Perhaps the most important qualification is CK's concluding "reminder" that the epistemic "levels" they describe are really "just convenient points along a continuum," and "for any individual believer, the location of any particular claim along that continuum is subject to revision in light of new arguments, new experiences, and new discoveries" (134-35).

This concluding observation provides a helpful entrée for my own response to CK's interesting proposal. CK are absolutely right to insist on two things: (1) the importance of looking for good reasons on which to base our beliefs, and (2) the fact that there is no single standard of rationality for belief. This presents us with an enormous challenge. Religious beliefs embody claims of enormous variety. There are metaphysical claims (claims about ultimate reality), historical claims, ethical claims, even psychological and emotional claims.

Consequently, I appreciate CK's attempt to provide a nuanced, highly varied account of justification. There is no one standard of rationality that applies to the full range of religious beliefs, any more than there is a single standard of rationality that applies to any significant area of human life.[4]

At the same time, I prefer the expression "continuum" to that of "levels," which pervades CK's discussion. The latter sets up a hierarchy of justification, or rationality, according to which some types of justification are higher than others, so that beliefs descend (119), decline (120), even fall (126) from higher to lower levels of justification. In light of our root cognitive metaphor that "good is up,"[5] the connotation is unavoidable that even though evidence of a highly personal nature may qualify as "rational," or justified to a degree, it is decidedly inferior to evidence of a public nature.

Instead of a hierarchical arrangement of rationality, I prefer that we place the various forms of justification at different locations on more or less the same level. This would allow us to regard beliefs that rely on different sorts of evidence—public *and* private evidence, for example—to be equally acceptable even though they derive from different sources. And it would allow people who hold a particular belief for different reasons to be equally rational in doing so.

Human Rationality—Universally Constitutive or a Wager?

On the other hand, I believe there is a rather important level of rationality, or form of rationality, to use the expression I prefer, that CK dismiss rather casually on page 119. There they assert that the argument that ultimate reality (UR) must share at least some human values is not a hypothesis at all but a judgment about something human agents must assume if they are to make sense of their own rational agency. Since we can't prove that human rational agency isn't finally based on an illusion, they say, it represents a wager or a bet.

To the contrary, in my view, to demonstrate that a belief is intrinsic to the very notion of rationality is to provide a most convincing form of justification. Such a belief is self-evidently true. It cannot fail to be true because it is part of the very meaning of truth. Or, to put it another way, it is a belief that cannot be doubted, because it is presupposed in every intellectual operation. It is intrinsic to the fabric of cognition.

This self-referential argument assumes a more sophisticated form in what is generally described as "transcendental philosophy." According to the dictionary definition, transcendental philosophy examines "the a priori conditions of knowledge, which precede all experience of objects and which are the primary constituents of all objects of knowledge and hence make knowledge possible."[6] Transcendental philosophers explore the foundations of knowledge as such, both scientific and philosophical, and they hold that no account of knowledge will do unless it takes into account "the thinker's own act of knowing."[7] Dispense with the knower, therefore, and you have eliminated any basis for knowledge, any confidence in what the knower claims to know.

Some things are therefore self-evidently true because they cannot be doubted. Every imaginable experience confirms them. No matter what I experience, for example, I cannot doubt my existence as the one who has these experiences. If I doubt, I cannot doubt that I am doubting. A philosophy student once asked a famous professor, "How do I know I exist?" The man answered, "And who is asking the question?" The question is self-answering. The very fact that you can ask the question means that you have an answer for it.

Human experience, then, exhibits great complexity, and different modes of experience require different forms of inquiry. Science explores the details of experience, the things that come and go. It does not deal with the permanent features of experience. But it is nevertheless possible to explore these features and account for them. Just as we use human experience, refined through instruments, to arrive at truth about the physical world, we can use human experience, refracted through careful analysis, to arrive at truth about the nature of reality as such, or reality as a whole. Whatever the whole show is, it has produced us; we are just as much a part of things as supernovas, monkeys, protozoans, and electrons. Consequently, we can look to our own experience for clues about the ultimate nature of things.[8]

Doubt *and* Trust

If there are possibilities for stronger arguments than CK acknowledge here, there are also reasons to question whether scientific standards deserve the status they seem to accord them. I have three observations to make in this connection. First of all, there are two paths to truth, not just one. Science seems to privilege the function of doubt. We are entitled to a belief only when we have overcome the relevant doubts connected with it.[9] When it comes to human knowledge, however, God has given us two gifts, both of which are important in our quest for truth. One is the ability to doubt; the other is the ability to trust. Without the ability to doubt, we would be completely gullible. We would believe anything anybody said. We would be easily fooled. Much worse, we would put ourselves in great danger. We wouldn't be able to tell good ideas from bad ones. We wouldn't know a right decision from a wrong one. In short, we would be incapable of rational investigation. The ability to doubt is very important.

Although in the eyes of many people, doubt is the most prominent feature in human knowing, it is not the only one. Trust is important, too. To know things, you also have to have trust. Sometimes we place our trust in other people. Sometimes we trust ourselves. We trust what our senses tell us about the world. We also trust the operation of our minds. Paradoxically, we even trust when we doubt. We trust the importance of doubt, we trust our minds to raise the right doubts, and we trust them to answer these doubts in a helpful way. We also trust ourselves to realize when we have doubted enough and come to the place where we can affirm something. So, without trust we would never come to knowledge.

So, trust and doubt represent two facets of human knowing. They also represent two responsibilities. We have the duty to avoid error. Doubt is essential for that. We also have the responsibility to embrace truth. Trust is important for that. The challenge of course is to fulfill both responsibilities. If we only had to avoid error, we could simply doubt everything, and we would never make a mistake. But that would paralyze us. On the other hand, if all we had to do were to embrace truth, then we would believe everything. But in that case, we would make all kinds of mistakes. The big question is how to balance the two, how to bring them together in a way that allows each one the right role in our thinking.

Not insignificantly, one gift is more prominent than the other at certain stages of life. Children are notoriously trusting. They are inclined to believe anything you tell them. Adolescents are notoriously skeptical. They are inclined to reject anything you tell them. There was a time when people said we should never trust anyone older than thirty. Of course, the people who said that are now in their sixties or seventies.

It is also the case that one of these gifts, trust and doubt, is more prominent than the other at certain times in history. Historians sometimes speak of the Middle Ages as the age of faith. With few exceptions, for about a thousand years in the Western world everyone held a religious view of things. And they got their beliefs from accepted authorities. From the Enlightenment onward, however, everything changed, and the prevalent attitude of people in the Western world became one of doubt. An intellectually responsible person today is instinctively skeptical. He or she doesn't accept any claims unless they can overcome objections and reservations.

In the world we live in, the supreme accomplishment of human reason is modern science, a marvelous combination of careful reflection and careful observation. Scientists make observations, formulate theories, and develop experiments to test these theories. Before any theory can be accepted, it has to square with the facts. So, it is not surprising that the "predicament of belief," according to the opening sentence of the book (vii), involves those who are committed to the values of "scientific rationality" and yet moved by the claims of a religious tradition.

None of us can escape the influence of scientific rationality. We all benefit from science and none of us would choose to live in a prescientific age. Science has increased our understanding and prolonged our lives. It is an enormous blessing and we should be grateful for it. So effective is science, and so impressive and beneficial are its achievements, that many people give science the last word on everything. In their view, an intellectually responsible person is someone who bases his or her beliefs on science. Unless something makes sense in scientific terms, they insist, unless there is empirical evidence to support it, we have no business believing it.

People who hold such a strong view of science are typically skeptical when it comes to religion, because religion makes claims, or certainly seems to make claims, for which scientific evidence is lacking. As they see it, we have to make a choice between science and religion, between reason and faith, and there is no question as to what the choice should be. I agree with CK that we do not have to choose between religion and science. It is perfectly possible to be religiously committed and intellectually responsible. Faith and reason are not opposed to each other. Both are important and both have a place in the life of the believer.

Beyond Science

Notwithstanding its importance and its influence, there are several features of science itself that require us to look beyond it.

(1) Science operates by doubt, and doubt has its limits. As Michael Polanyi notes, there are limits to the effectiveness of this approach to truth.

Doubt is not the path to all truth. "Today we should be grateful for the prolonged attacks made by rationalists on religion for forcing us to renew the grounds of the Christian faith. But this does not remotely justify the acknowledgment of doubt as the universal solvent of error that will leave truth untouched behind.

For all truth is but the external pole of belief, and to destroy all belief would be to deny all truth."[10]

Religious beliefs are similar to certain mathematical and scientific truths. "The specification of [religious] beliefs is much more colourful than are the axioms of arithmetic or the premises of natural science. But they belong to the same class of statements, performing kindred fiduciary functions."[11]

The way of doubt obscures the range of knowledge. "Objectivism has totally falsified our conception of truth, by exalting what we can know and prove, while covering up with ambiguous utterance all that we know and *cannot* prove, even though the latter knowledge underlies, and must ultimately set its seal to, all that we *can* prove. In trying to restrict our minds to the few things that are demonstrable, and therefore explicitly dubitable, it has overlooked the critical choices which determine the whole being of our minds and has rendered us incapable of acknowledging these vital choices."[12]

(2) There are *practical* limitations to the applicability of science.

Sometimes the demand for conclusive evidence is impossible to meet. There are situations where we have to make decisions with less than a clear preponderance of evidence to guide us.

Sometimes the demand for conclusive evidence is impractical. Our everyday reliance on common sense expresses a confidence in the trustworthiness of the world around us, physical and social. We could not get through the day if we subjected every belief to the scrutiny of a scientific inquiry.

Sometimes the demand for conclusive evidence is destructive. Love and friendship rest on trust. A persistent demand for proof would destroy the fabric of trust on which these relationships rest. We would have no friends if we demanded proof for every assertion other people made.

(3) Scientific inquiry rests on convictions that science presupposes but does not and cannot prove.

The scientific ethic. The discovery of truth depends on certain qualities in the seeker for truth. The scientist at his/her best is committed to pursuing truth, modest in his/her claims to have found the truth, and careful to use the truth only in ways that will benefit humankind. Science thus presupposes an ethic on the part of scientists that is "nonscientific," or "prescientific."

The presuppositions of science. The activity of science, as well as the behavior of scientists, rests on assumptions that are non-scientific (not unscientific). Scientists exhibit a version of "faith," confidence in certain unproven (and unprovable) convictions: (a) the world is real; (b) the world makes sense; it is humanly understandable; (c) the world is worth the trouble it takes to understand it.

Immanuel Kant once said that he destroyed reason in order to make room for faith. To a certain extent we have been doing that here. Not destroying reason, but trying to look carefully at the contours or the outlines of reason. Reason is indispensable to human knowing. But the process of rational, deliberate investigation, which looks carefully at every claim and overcomes all possible objections before accepting an idea, has its limits.

Two concluding comments. Scientific cosmology presents us with a challenging choice. There is a radical disjunction between two irreconcilable views of ourselves. Either human beings are *creation's crowning glory,* or we are *nature's cruelest joke.* For the universe to have produced at last beings whose distinctive quality is their capacity to see that reality has no meaning, no purpose, and no future for them is the height of irony. On the other hand, suppose the apprehension of meaning, value, and significance in ourselves and in the world is veridical. Suppose it reflects and corresponds to the Ultimate Reality who has brought us into existence. Here is the crucial question: *Are we at home in the universe or aren't we?* That is the great alternative that confronts us. Science alone cannot answer that question. We must turn to religion for an answer, and what to do with that answer is something that faith will ultimately decide.

A final response to CK's proposal concerns the power of personal or private evidence. As a Christian, of course, I find the figure of Jesus Christ central to my understanding of God and human existence. And I find the influence of this figure irresistible. It is not hard to understand, given my experience as a lifelong Seventh-day Adventist. But I think there are other reasons to view Jesus as the major influence for good in human history. Then, too, there are accounts of people who find Jesus remarkably attractive, in contrast to all reasonable expectation. For example, consider my friend, an Israeli tour guide. Born in Israel to survivors of the Holocaust, he went to Rome to study biology. Growing up in Israel he had heard of Jesus, of course, but in Rome he felt surrounded with all the churches, statues, and religious figures. So he decided to learn something more about the object of all the attention. As I recall his account, reading the Sermon on the Mount was a life-changing experience. This, he was convinced, was the way human beings were meant to live. Instead of biology, he made theology the object of his graduate study, eventually earning an MTh from the Pontifical Gregorian University. Along the way he also taught classes in Hebrew at the Greg to his fellow students.

Whatever conclusions we reach on the basis of careful scientific, historical, and philosophical examination—and I am not for a moment underestimating their importance or their value—I believe that our hearts will always want something more. And that is what the

Gospel of Jesus Christ provides. As the prologue of the fourth Gospel concludes, "No one has ever seen God. It is God the only Son—who is close to the Father's heart—who has made him known."

---

[1] Gary Dorrien, *The Making of American Liberal Theology: Crisis, Irony, and Postmodernity, 1950-2005* (Louisville: Westminster John Knox Press, 2006), 535-7.

[2] For example, I once heard Don Cuppitt of Cambridge University make this remarkable statement: "I don't believe that God exists, but I pray every day, using words from the Book of Common Prayer." Cf. "Our most fundamental beliefs have simply to be chosen. Their 'truth' is not descriptive or factual truth, but the truth about the way they work out in our lives." Don Cuppitt, *The Sea of Faith* (New York: Cambridge University Press, 1984), 19.

[3] E.g. Colin Powell's decision not to run for the Presidency.

[4] Note for example, the different evidential criteria employed in American jurisprudence. To convict a defendant of a crime, the prosecution must establish guilt beyond a reasonable doubt and to a moral certainty. (Note: the doubt must be reasonable, not wildly hypothetical, such as the notion that an alien clone of the defendant actually committed the crime.) For someone to be found responsible for damages in a civil case, however, a preponderance of evidence is sufficient.

[5] Cf. George Lakoff and Mark Johnson, *Metaphors We Live By* (Chicago: University of Chicago Press, 1980).

[6] Hans Michael Baumgartner, "Transcendental Philosophy," in *Encyclopedia of Theology: The Concise Sacramentum Mundi,* ed. Karl Rahner (New York: Seabury, 1975), 1743.

[7] Baumgartner, 1745.

[8] Consequently, we are not left with scientific facts on the one hand and pure subjectivity on the other. Our own experience provides evidence to support metaphysical claims, or descriptions of ultimate reality. The fact that such evidence is different from the empirical evidence in which science traffics and requires its own mode of inquiry does not mean that it is a matter of mere personal preference.

[9] Cf. Popper's criterion of falsifiability.

[10] Michael Polanyi, *Personal Knowledge: Towards a Post-Critical Philosophy* (Chicago: University of Chicago Press, 1958), 286.

[11] Ibid.

[12] Ibid.

8
STRICTLY RATIONAL BELIEF MISSES THE GENUIS OF RELIGION

A Reflection on Chapter 8, "The Spectrum of Belief and the Question of the Church"

James W. Walters

The Predicament of Belief sets a new standard as a concise, insightful summary of the poignant challenges to Christian faith by contemporary thought in five areas—science, evil, plurality of world religions, critical biblical scholarship, and the Resurrection. Clayton and Knapp (hereafter CK) have a method that reminds one of good debate preparation: know your opponent's case as well as your own. But these authors go a step further in summarizing the opposition's case in persuasive terms that are beyond the capabilities of many skeptics. This approach laudably bespeaks the authors' openness, scholarship, and honesty, but I will argue that CK don't win the battle of belief because their critique is not sufficiently religious in its attempt to meet skeptics on their own ground.

Our authors' goal is to make the Christian faith logically acceptable to well-read Christians and intellectually plausible to secular people. In earlier works Clayton has essentially said to readers, "Show me where I am wrong as I truly want to learn, and I will change." Here CK yield, up front, on such issues as Jesus being the equivalent of God herself and routine miracles, quite easily accepting that these traditional beliefs do not sustain contemporary examination. Like wise generals, CK drop back to a supposedly defensible trench, and make the strongest case possible for the faith, although it's an admittedly minimalist faith (and not for everyone). This is not an evangelistic ploy but an almost joyful affirmation of the advance of knowledge (truth) on multiple fronts, which demands a correlated advance in theology. Here CK are but following the footsteps of the modern father of correlative theology, Paul Tillich.[1]

CK are bold in laying out the scientific and historical challenges to belief, and they are equally bold in assessing Jesus' resurrection in light of contemporary thought—all in preparation for the practical issue of how the church can thrive in today's world. This book is a sophisticated construction of contemporary, practical theology. Thus, in this final chapter, it is only appropriate that the authors focus on themes of resurrection and church. In this essay, however, I question the adequacy of the authors' cognitive, belief-based emphasis (illustrated by their focus on resurrection) for the contemporary church.

Resurrection and its Rationality

Jesus' Resurrection, "the heart of the predicament this book was designed to address," occupies a quarter of the chapters. Its reality is a logical extension of CK's undergirding argument that the Ultimate Reality is not less than personal, would therefore want the existence of self-actualizing beings, and would desire personal communication— all without violating the natural laws that necessarily underlie morally responsible human life. In this vein CK offer a revisionist idea of the Resurrection: it was a non-physical personal event that demonstrated the self-giving love of Jesus and makes possible our ongoing participation in a human-divine relationship not previously available. Here CK see Paul's vision of Jesus on the Damascus road as paradigmatic for the resurrected Christ who is available to believers today, just as he was to the apostle.

Paul acknowledged Jesus' post-resurrection appearances to the disciples, but his focus was on Christ's later appearance to himself, one that came in a flash of light and was unique. That risen Christ is not so much a lone individual as a continuation of Christ's life-giving righteousness: "Anyone who does not have the Spirit of Christ does not belong to him..." (Rom 8:9). CK believe that Paul portrayed the Resurrection as the event that established a "new mode of divine-human relationship" and that is why Paul so freely interchanges the terms Christ, Spirit of Christ, Spirit of God, and Spirit. CK discount the gospels' accounts of the resurrection due to the scientific implausibility of a resuscitation. They see significant conflicts among the various accounts of those appearances, for example, the conflicting accounts of Jesus' first appearing to a variety of individuals—alternately the assembled disciples, Peter, Mary Magdalene, the two Marys, and two unnamed disciples (84).

Our authors realize the intellectual difficulty of belief in Jesus' Resurrection, and they deal with it, in part, by distinguishing among several levels of justification of belief that we employ in our religious and everyday lives. But their focus is conscious "belief," despite the fact that most people most of the time function on the basis of largely unexamined but crucial assumptions, such as the significance of life. The great majority of us get up every morning with the sense that our lives are meaningful, although any so-called "proof" of this assumption is thin.

Perhaps the most significant benefit of this book is CK's delineation of levels of justification of beliefs. They identify and embrace six levels of belief, an insightful acceptance that we humans do and should hold certain beliefs more dearly than we do others. They attempt to make sense of this reality, because humans are complex and inconsistent and legitimately hold both rational and non-rational beliefs.

The six degrees or levels of justification of beliefs are:

(1) One's belief is endorsed by the relevant community of experts (RCE), or it will be once the RCE can evaluate one's reasons for the belief.

(2) One's belief is *not* endorsed by the RCE, and endorsement is not expected. But one thinks that the RCE's view could be corrected, due to a remediable error.

(3) One's belief is *not* endorsed by the RCE, and endorsement is not expected. One does *not* think that the RCE's can be corrected because there is no specific mistake in the RCE's reasoning. Thus the belief is "irreducibly controversial." Yet one's life experience and position are good reasons for the belief.

(4) One's belief is the same as (3), but the belief is ambiguous to oneself—given serious criticisms and the unclear experiences from which one reasons. One no longer sees her beliefs as rationally *indicated*, only as rationally *permissible*.

(5) One *hopes* that her desire will eventually be proven to be true, but is currently only a "seeker."

(6) One does not believe as most would define the term, but does accept metaphorical terms that indicate an ultimate reality that might exist.

This schema is directly related to the Resurrection because traditionally Christians have thought of resurrection and other core Christian ideas as beliefs that must be accepted as simply true, without nuance. Some people whose names are on church rosters no longer consider themselves Christian, because they no longer simply believe proposition x or y. The genius of CKs' book is that they accept, even laud, the advance in knowledge, even when that very knowledge makes some traditional religious tenets obsolete or in need of serious revision. Resurrection is one such belief, and CK recognize and even appreciate the plurality of Christians' positions: literal belief, mere hope, suspended disbelief, hope-plus-faith, metaphorical belief, and behaving-as-if. Such diversity should be expected in light of the controversial nature of the church's claim that its original teacher was resurrected. In keeping with their case for minimalist faith, CK define the Resurrection as a "profoundly and literally *spiritual* event" (139, CK's emphasis).

CK themselves view the Resurrection as possessing level-3 justification: the Resurrection is admittedly controversial (as relevant experts do not agree), but belief is justified due to the personal assumptions and experiences that a believer brings to the issue. They posit a level-2 justification for belief in God's existence, evidently the type of superior intelligence behind the marvel of DNA that prompted the late and famous atheist Anthony Flew to change his mind. But whether belief in a not-less-than-personal God has this level of evidence is less clear. At times CK seem to suggest that the Resurrection ushered in a relationship with God heretofore unavailable, and if this were the case, the difficulty of justifying this claim would involve, at minimum, demonstrating that none of the millions of believers pre-Resurrection realized the close relationship to God that two thousand years ago became categorically available to subsequent believers. Thus this latter belief would likely slip to level 4 in justification.

Religion as beyond Science: Buber, Toulmin, and Tracy

The intention of CK is laudable—to make the Christian story credible to the contemporary world of the well informed, and these authors make a good case for meeting objections by restricting the number of beliefs they must defend and lowering the level of justification needed to defend others. But is the core issue really about specific beliefs, specifiable evidence, and counter-evidence? I think not. CK are at the top of their Wittgensteinian game of demonstrating how cold logic can conclude a not-less-than-personal God, given plausible decisions at key junctures in their logic of belief. But this game, helpful as it is to some, misses the point that there is another approach, related but distinguishable, that is more basic and largely missing here— the profoundly *religious* dimension of reality that exists beyond the evidential game that science plays.[2]

As a concept, "belief," a largely rationalistic idea, has significant but finally limited scope in exploration of the predicament of faith. The authors themselves implicitly acknowledge this in their pronounced nuancing of the term throughout the book. In this chapter alone they suggest that belief can "oscillate" between weaker and stronger forms (140), can "vacillate between clear belief and hope-plus-faith," and can be unreserved or metaphorical (146). Belief deals with acceptance of whether a statement is true or something exists, according the dictionary. Without question, the issue of truthful assertions and of the existence of things is important, but it isn't fully adequate to the discourse needed to explore the significance of existence itself—Ultimate Reality.

And here I will draw on the thought of three diverse thinkers to illumine this larger dimension: the Jewish thinker Martin Buber, philosopher Steven Toulmin, and Christian theologian David Tracy.

Martin Buber, the Jewish writer who referred to himself as a religious thinker, eschewing the term "theologian" as indicating a systematization he rejected as inadequate and criticized Pauline Christianity for its focus on *belief*, choosing what he saw as the touchstone of Hebraic religion—*trust*. Buber portrays Christianity as concerned for the lone individual, separated from any historic community, who is called to believe in a less than rational gospel, whereas Judaism is called to trust in the everlasting God. "The crisis of our time is also the crisis of two types of faith, Emunah and Pistis. They are as fundamentally different in nature as in their origin, and accordingly their crisis is different. The origin of the Jewish Emunah is in the history of a nation, that of Christian Pistis in that of individuals. Emunah originated in the actual experiences of Israel, which were to it experiences of faith."[3] The key point for this discussion is Buber's recognition of the rich social contextualization of our individual lives, in contrast to the neutered individualism Buber found in Pauline Christianity—and that continues in strains of today's Protestantism.

A related but distinguishable examination of initial assumptions is advanced by Stephen Toulmin, who argues that religion and science are not dealing with the same issues or, put differently, that they are assessing life at different levels of abstraction. Science deals with things that can be measured and with laws that can be demonstrated through replicable experiments, and religion deals with matters of final significance. "Over matters of faith, one does not 'believe' or 'disbelieve' individual propositions," says Toulmin, "one 'accepts' or 'rejects' complete notions. Indeed, we might describe the distinction between 'faith' and 'reason' in these terms—belief as a matter of reason is *belief of* a proposition of some kind; belief as a matter of faith is *belief in* a notion of some kind."[4]

Toulmin uses belief in God as an illustration: One must first accept the "notion of 'God'" and only then is one in a position to point to evidence of His existence. CK echo a similar point in saying that often today's inquirers participate in a church community and come to share its values *before* coming to belief (147). Toulmin shows the vital prior role of context and assumptions, as he contends that "The very last question to ask about God is whether he exists." He makes his point by quoting from Pascal:

> The heart and the mind both have their method. That of the mind is according to principle and demonstration; that of the heart is otherwise. One does not show that one ought to be loved by setting forth in order the causes of love: that would be ridiculous. Jesus Christ and St. Paul have the method of charity, not of the intellect; for they wished to enkindle, not instruct.

And Toulmin then adds:

> By this [Pascal] reminds us that, when we are discussing matters of religion, we must seek less for a rational demonstration than for evidences of their truth; and that it would be misunderstanding the purpose of religion and the nature of religious "truth"—and so in a sense self-contradictory—to demand an answer obtained literally, by "the method of intellect," to a question meant spiritually and calling for "the method of the heart."[5]

Life's really big issues are addressed by one's whole being, not just logical cognition; that's the way we do and should approach these issues. Literal, naked, individual, belief is too narrow a category—*especially* in light of contemporary neuroscience.

Toulmin's idea of "limiting" questions (questions that can be addressed by scientific analysis, but finally transcend such scrutiny—e.g., a tree exhaustively studied by a botanist, and still inspiring *wonder*) was an impetus, in part, for David Tracy to distinguish "limit-to" and "limit-of" dimensions of human experience: "All genuine limit-situations refer to those experiences, both positive and negative, wherein we both experience our own human limits (limit-to) as our own as well as recognize, however haltingly, some disclosure of a limit of our experience." The two dimensions of experience are related, but the latter is more profound in signaling a religious dimension that's not in competition with science, logic, morality, etc., but that begins to address them all in their ontological significance. This dimension acts "as a final, now gracious, now frightening, now trustworthy, now absurd, always uncontrollable limit—of the very meaning of existence itself."[6] For want of a better term to describe the above Buberian-Toulminian-Tracian approach to issues of religion's very being, I'll call it *existential*.

CK distinguish their approach to the predicament of belief from alternatives: Christian agnosticism, symbolism, faith supplementing reason, and "religious feeling or religious 'experience' as something that is both more elusive and more fundamental than anything one can reason about" (4). They say that, intentional or not, the tendency of all these approaches is to *"immunize"* Christian claims from skeptics. This criticism doesn't fit the existential approach indicated above. However, the existential approach does underscore a dimension of life that undergirds all explicit religious claims, and it can be reasoned about, although it finally recognizes the limits to all rational enterprises. Such modesty itself is reasonable, given that the subject is God—thus indicating an appropriate role for Christian mysticism.

Beyond the Public/Private Evidence Duality

My colleague Rick Rice, in the previous essay in this book, appropriately indicates the privileged position CK give to *rational* justification, as determined by society's relevant experts. But he disagrees with the formulation:

> Instead of a hierarchical arrangement of rationality I prefer that we place the various forms of justification at different locations on more or less the same level. This would allow us to regard beliefs that rely on different sorts of evidence—public *and* private evidence, for example—to be equally acceptable even though they derive from different sources. And it would allow people who hold a particular belief for different reasons to be equally rational in doing so.[7]

CK's hierarchical levels do privilege the low numbered ranks: #1 (one's belief is confirmed by relevant experts) is preferable to #6 (one's belief is rejected by experts and finally by oneself). Rice accepts the fundamental differences we humans have in personal histories, aesthetics, aptitudes, personalities, etc., and he understandably wants equality in what he calls public and private evidence. But equally privileging the two loses a valuable point of CK's hierarchy: that application of disciplined, accumulated human intelligence among the academy's experts matters. It's CK's lack of attention to the existential level at which we live—consciously and more often subconsciously making choices, and having choices made for us by parents and society—that may have led to their leveling of the existential and rational levels of human experience. At its best, Rice's position allows each person to make her best case for how she draws on both private and public evidence in constructing a defensible worldview. At worst, it is open to the criticism of relativism, allowing idiosyncratic individuals to mix personal views and pubic evidence in reprehensible fashion.

Rather than CK's general privileging of public evidence and Rice's equality of public and private perspectives, a more defensible scenario will only be briefly sketched: 1) *Existential life positions* as determined by self, others, and nature; 2) *objective evidence* as determined by society's relevant experts; and 3) *personal choice* about how to appropriate objective evidence in light of one's existentially given life. I suggest that this three-stage scenario is a description of how we humans actually do found our lives, justify our beliefs, and chart our lives in regard to religion and also in regard to our lives in general. In a very truncated fashion, I indicate how this approach might function.

Existential life. Our lives are largely determined by our genetic, social, and historical lotteries. We individually had nothing to do with the pool of genes that so control our lives. Similarly, we had nothing to do with the parents to whom we were born. And of course, we didn't choose to be born in the twentieth century. Beyond these huge existential factors, there are big questions about life that are finally answered, in the most optimal circumstances, by choices we make about our worldviews and how we will chart our lives. It is finally up to us to decide whether our individual lives are meaningful in any ultimate sense, given the minute speck our planet is in the universe. Is there a God at all, to say nothing of the *biblical* God? Why am I here? Where am I going?

We as individuals answer these questions, often implicitly, by living according to the conventions we have been taught. But the key point is that we do not simply believe *x* about these matters and make decisions based on demonstrable evidence.

Objective Evidence. Society appropriately functions on the assumption that human life is eminently meaningful, and the vast majority of individuals share that assumption. The fact that this assumption of life's meaningfulness is ubiquitous does not belie its being based on less than demonstrable evidence. However, given this common, shared conviction, it makes sense to subsequently, but surely, privilege public, objective evidence. Rational persons must ask: what do those who have deeply and systematically explored an area of knowledge say about their area of expertise? Public evidence is comprised of the accumulation of experts' knowledge. Objective evidence is relevant in addressing such questions as:

- Is evolutionary theory or biblical creationism more credible?
- Is it true that Christians are morally superior to secular folk?
- Is there unanimity in the New Testament on Jesus' resurrection?

Personal choice. Beyond availing oneself of the objective evidence available on myriad topics, the decision of *how* to weigh conflicting evidence and *how* to factor in one's existential situation and one's private desires is a personal matter—and *should* be.

What does all this have to do with the Resurrection? The scenario of Existential Life, Objective Evidence, and Personal Choice puts the Resurrection discussion into a larger frame of reference, as issues surrounding Resurrection primarily make sense to the person who is existentially interested. The six-level gradient of belief justification is tailor-made for an in-church discussion of the Resurrection, and it allows for a variety of views. But its restricted focus on belief, as important as that discussion is for questions such as resurrection, can belie the grander, existential role that religion and spirituality play in human lives.

The Challenge of Church Today

This book has a practical purpose—to make the gospel credible to modern/postmodern society and attract an increasingly skeptical public to Christian churches. In comments to the religious studies class that was the impetus for this volume, Philip Clayton said that he is turning from writing erudite books steeped in theoretical science and continental philosophy to writing books for the lay public.[8] It is not coincidental that the concluding chapter of the original *Predicament* book concerns the church and how it can attract postmodern folk. Neither is it coincidental that Clayton at the time this essay was written was Dean of Claremont School of Theology, which is affiliated with the United Methodist Church, and in early 2012 wrote an op-ed piece for the *Los Angeles Times* on the doubting church whose graphic was a traditional church with a steeple topped off by a question-mark, not a cross.[9]

In being honest about traditional Christian belief, in light of contemporary knowledge, Clayton was compelled to join co-author Steven Knapp in embracing a minimally personalistic theism and they proceeded to construct a concomitant minimalist resurrection. Further, the authors of this book were attracted to a minimalist version of Christianity because of current trends they observed in the Western world:

(1) The church is no longer necessary for social cohesion and formation of business and career relationships.

(2) Few people now see church attendance as the most important means of establishing and maintaining a relationship with God.

(3) The dramatically increased mobility of individuals and families and greater instability of family units make extended ties to a church community difficult.

(4) Christians are much more diverse in beliefs, values, and social identities than in past eras, and thus maintaining a critical mass of congregants is difficult.

(5) Seventy two percent of Millennials (essentially twenty-somethings) view themselves as "spiritual but not religious."

(6) Less than 1% of Germans attend church on any given Sunday, and American church attendance is on the decline.

The modern day challenge to Christian belief goes even further than CK observe, if sociologist of religion Phil Zuckerman is correct:

> If there is an earthly heaven for secular folk, contemporary Denmark and Sweden may very well be it: quaint towns, inviting cities, beautiful forests, lonely beaches, healthy democracies, among the lowest violent crime rates in the world, the lowest levels of corruption in in the world, excellent educational systems, innovative architecture, strong economies, well supported arts, successful entrepreneurship, clean hospitals, delicious beer, free health care, maverick filmmaking, egalitarian social policies, sleek design, comfortable bike paths—and not much faith in God.[10]

Statistics bear out Zuckerman's generalizations: Sweden ranks sixth in life expectancy; Sweden and Denmark, along with four other nations, have the lowest infant mortality rates. In gender equality, Denmark and Sweden rank second and third, respectively. In lack of corruption among public officials, Denmark is fourth and Sweden is sixth. In charity to poor nations, Denmark ranks second, and Sweden third.[11]

Both Denmark and Sweden are world leaders in many indices of social success, but what about their inner lives? A commonplace assumption among sociologists of religion is that humans yearn for meaning in life (Stark, Bainbridge, Berger, Greeley, Pargament, Weber, and others). But Zuckerman tells a different story:

> Based on my research among Danes and Swedes, I have started to theorize that most people, most of the time—at least in certain cultures—don't actually worry too much or actually even care about the "ultimate meaning of life." What probably concerns most people most of the time are things like their job (or lack thereof), their family life, what they are going to eat, their friends, sex, the neighbor's barking dog, etc.[12]

Zuckerman, an acknowledged atheist, may not be entirely objective in his collection and analysis of data, but nonetheless his results further underscore the need for books such as *The Predicament of Belief*.

One would think that sophisticated Western Europeans, particularly Scandinavians, would be candidates for a type of emergent church experience—a strong Lutheran background, educated, and open-minded. If churches anywhere in the world were open to a plurality of congregants, Scandinavian churches would appear likely candidates. But radical openness isn't swelling the attendance at divine services in Sweden or Denmark. And if a Claytonian type church doesn't make it in Scandinavia, where might it succeed? Perhaps in America, where church attendance is still amazingly high, compared to attendance rates in other highly industrialized nations. But in North America today, mainline denominations have become old line, and fundamentalist-type churches are the fastest growing. In early 2012 there was a Rock Church billboard on the 10 freeway only five miles west of Loma Linda that read: "NO BULL. ONLY THE TRUTH."[13]

The CK perspective on Christian faith is broadly ecumenical in its "Christian proposition": "that the infinite grace and compassion of the Ultimate Reality itself were present, and *in some sense* continue to be present, in this particular human being [Jesus]" (141), and it should be broad. But CK's minimalist faith is not for everyone, e.g., the Rock Church.

Whereas there is room in CK's church for left-of-center seekers, there is also room for right-of-center believers—there must be. I think of the immigrant handyman, let's call him Carlos, who has aided me in housework for several years. Carlos only has six years of formal education, but speaks and writes English better than many of his friends who have high school diplomas. Because of his varied work in construction and his native intelligence, he is adept at everything from building rock walls to changing out shower valves. Carlos was physically and emotionally abused as a child, but is slowly growing in self-esteem—in part because of his heightened interest in religion (he now only listens to Christian radio as he works around the yard). And when Carlos plies me with questions such as "Did I really come from a monkey?" or "Do you believe that the Second Coming is just around the corner?" I must be careful not to impose on him the rarified spiritual air I need to thrive.

The CK notion of an ideal church seems to be one that has joyful members, knee-to-knee, possessing a variety of religious ideologies: Christian fideist and agnostic, the merely hopeful and those with suspended disbelief, those with metaphorical belief and others behaving-as-if. And although CK don't emphasize them, the church has many more members who are scriptural literalists, whose only good word for the week is the preacher's simple gospel, and who are totally put off by "bickering" over the Holy Bible. The church of Christ must be radically inclusive, left and right, and Group Dynamics 101 dictates that different congregations for different types of Christians is a necessity to meet legitimate human need.

That said, CK are leading the way to ensure that the historical media of our faith, so valued by some, don't repulse others: "Above all, the church should never fear the truth, because its very existence only matters if the truth is what it teaches" (154). No fools, CK recognize the cost of their revisionist narrative of Christian faith, but they see no choice. The challenge is clear:

> Why should people continue to stake their lives on a tradition whose claims are subject to revision in light of new information? [H]ow can one continue to be moved, inspired, and spiritually uplifted by an ancient miracle story that has now been revised in a way that downplays or even removes the dimension of miracle, at least as miracles are conventionally understood? (138)

What do CK have to offer our post-Christian society? A religiously democratic church, one open to all stripes of believers and seekers alike. They are to be applauded for their insightful, bold attempt to rescue the church for a postmodern generation. For fifteen centuries preceding the Enlightenment we believed; today, as portrayed in the title of Charles Taylor's influential book, we live in "a secular age."[14] Yet the relevance of the Christian proposition endures: God's infinite grace and compassion continue in some sense to be manifest in Jesus.

---

[1] Paul Tillich's initial "method of correlation," developed in his *Systematic Theology*, vol. 1 (Chicago: University of Chicago Press, 1951), posed society's existential questions and responded with theological/biblical answers. In the subsequent decades the concept of correlative theology (not necessarily Tillich's particular poles) has significantly influenced theologians as diverse as Hans Küng, Rosemary Ruether, Schubert Ogden, David Tracy, and Philip Clayton. Clayton's correlative theology was clearly articulated in his inaugural address as Ingraham Professor, Claremont School of Theology: "The Many Faces of Integration: A New Vision for Liberal Theology (and for CST) between Church, Academy, and World," March 30, 2005, later published in his *Adventures in the Spirit: God, World, Divine Action* (Minneapolis: Fortress Press, 2008).

[2] If the domain of religion is eclipsed by scientific considerations, Clayton's involvement in science may be the reason, as he is one of the leading philosophers of religion and science, having begun publishing in the area with *Explanation from Physics to Theology* (New Haven: Yale University Press, 1989) and also notably co-edited the *Oxford Handbook of Religion and Science* (New York: Oxford University Press, 2006), in addition to other books and anthologies in the area.

[3] Martin Buber, *Two Types of Faith: A Study of the Interpretation of Judaism and Christianity*, trans. Norman Goldhawk (New York: Macmillan, 1951), 170. "Emunah is the state of 'preserving'—also to be called trust in the existential sense—of man in an invisible guidance which yet gives itself to be seen, in a hidden but self-revealing guidance...the personal Emunah of every individual remains embodied in that of the nation and draws its strength from the living memory of generations in the great leadings of early times." Whereas Buber is critical of the apostle Paul, he appreciates Jesus: "To be sure Jesus also addresses himself to the individual or, when he speaks to a number of people, to the individuals amongst them; but one has only to listen how (Matt. xv. 24) he speaks about the 'lost sheep of the house of Israel'; he sees even them still in the frame of the 'house'. The like is not heard after him. Paul often speaks about Jews and Greeks, but never in connexion with the reality of their nationalities..." (170, 172).

[4] Stephen Toulmin, *An Examination of the Place of Reason in Ethics* (Cambridge:

Cambridge University Press, 1950), 213 (emphasis is Toulmin's).

[5] Ibid., 214, 217.

[6] David Tracy, *Blessed Rage for Order: The New Pluralism in Theology* (New York: Seabury Press, 1975), 105, 108.

[7] Richard Rice, 129-130.

[8] Philip Clayton is passionate about revitalizing the church, and this passion was shared by the late Hans Frei, who emphasized the "plain sense" of scripture in his advocacy of a greater reading of the Bible within churches. But Frei was a Barthian, opposed correlative theology, and shared little in the way of theological approach with Philip Clayton.

[9] Philip Clayton, "Letting Doubters in the Door," *Los Angeles Times*, March 25, 2012.

[10] Phil Zuckerman, *Society without God: What the Least Religious Nations Can Tell Us about Contentment* (New York: New York University Press, 2008), 2-3.

[11] Ibid., 25-29.

[12] Ibid., 73.

[13] In 25 years this congregation has grown from twelve members to over 22,000, now spread over five campuses in inland southern California.

[14] Charles Taylor, *A Secular Age* (Cambridge, MA: Belknap Press, 2007).

PART II
A RESPONSE TO OUR CRITICS

PHILIP CLAYTON
AND STEVEN KNAPP

INTRODUCTION

The Predicament of Belief was written for people who are drawn to, or at least curious about, the possibility of religious, and particularly Christian, belief in the face of the many reasons for doubting that religious claims are actually true. We wrote the book in the hope of stimulating a broader conversation, one that would avoid the melodrama and polarization that have recently come to characterize debates about the conflict between religion and science, theism and atheism, traditional belief and modern skepticism. We are grateful, consequently, to each of our eight critics for taking the time, investing the effort, and manifesting the courage not only to respond to our book but to state their own doubts and concerns. They have begun a valuable dialogue, and for that reason we are in their debt.

In what follows, we have divided our reply to the eight essays into three responses, each addressing one central topical area. Response 1, "Participation and Emergence," answers the dual charges of reductionism and dualism. Some of our critics argue that our account of the human mind eliminates the soul and reduces the human person to mere "matter in motion"; others argue that we continue to treat human beings as both body and soul, thereby failing to do justice to the demands of modern science. These are both important charges. We anticipated them in chapters 3 and 5 of *Predicament*, but we did so only briefly. We agree that it is urgent to explain more carefully what is and is not entailed by emergent complexity as revealed by contemporary science.

Response 2, "Christ as 'Risen,'" takes on what is probably the most controversial claim of Christianity, today as much as in the century of its origin. Our critics have worried whether our position in *Predicament* allows for that personal connection to Jesus the Christ that has been so central to Christian experience throughout its history. We believe that our position preserves a place for this connection, and these pages show why, in somewhat more detail then we were able to offer in the book.

Response 3, "What Stance Do I Take toward My Own Beliefs?" addresses the important questions about doubt, knowledge, and faith that our critics have variously raised. In the book, we tried to show the viability of the various attitudes or stances that one may adopt toward the core Christian claims. Our critics have prompted us, however, to go further in presenting our own conclusions and in drawing more clearly the connection between what is believed and the manner in which one believes it.

A brief epilogue, "Seeking Belief and Community in an Age of Doubt," serves to round out our responses to the Loma Linda critics. Its main points are motivated by our concern for what these questions of belief and doubt actually mean for the current (and future) state of the church. During the nearly three decades that we have been struggling with finding responses to the major doubts about Christianity, the situation of the church has changed radically. Today even major church leaders are speaking openly of a crisis that some regard as destined to change the face of the institutional church as we have known it since the founding of this country. Few people can separate their reasons for doubt from their struggles with the church and the church's struggles with contemporary society. Personal faith and private spirituality are alive and well in the United States, but for many people, belonging to a religious community has become increasingly difficult. These issues have become so urgent today that they are now inseparable from the more general reasons for doubt that we explore in *Predicament.*

Even this extensive dialogue of eight critiques and four responses will not resolve all the questions that the authors are debating here. At most we can take a few further steps in an ongoing dialogue and then invite our readers to join us, whether as critics or supporters, in their own struggle with evolving belief in a rapidly evolving world.

9

RESPONSE 1

Participation an Emergence

A particular model of science, which many trace back to the time of Isaac Newton, interprets nature as a closed deterministic system. On this view, because everything that exists or occurs is a direct instance of a universal law, all future and past states of the universe could be deduced from a complete knowledge of those laws and the state of the universe at a given moment. This viewpoint is classically expressed in the thought experiment that has come to be known as "Laplace's Demon":

> We may regard the present state of the universe as the effect of its past and the cause of its future. An intellect which at a certain moment would know all forces that set nature in motion, and all positions of all items of which nature is composed, if this intellect were also vast enough to submit these data to analysis, it would embrace in a single formula the movements of the greatest bodies of the universe and those of the tiniest atom; for such an intellect nothing would be uncertain and the future just like the past would be present before its eyes.[1]

It turns out that this view of the universe is false. Scientists have discovered many features of natural processes that are incompatible with Laplace's mechanism: Heisenberg's Uncertainty Principle; quantum indeterminacy; sensitive dependence on initial conditions, also known as chaos theory; and the irreducibility of biological systems to systems of pure physics. These changes do not eliminate the distinctiveness of science or make it equivalent to the humanities. In studying human cognitive behavior, for example, scientists are able to establish amazing correlations between neural states and conscious experience. One should not underestimate how much more we will know about the relationship of the brain and human subjectivity in just ten or twenty years.

What systems biology does show, in contrast to (say) genetic reductionism, is that "nothing but" accounts are false. Early microbiologists liked to claim that proteins were "nothing but" the expressions of genes, and hence that everything that happened in cells, organs, brains, or even the organism as a whole was nothing but the product of "selfish genes."[2] We now know, however, that proteomics, the study of the sum total of protein interactions in a cell, cannot be reduced to genetic terms; to understand proteomics is to understand things that the science of genetics cannot fully explain. The same is true of metabolomics, the study of the sum total of metabolic reactions in a cell. This non-reducibility is true with a vengeance when it comes to inter-cellular interactions, immunology (the study of the immune responses of an organism), or the functioning of the central nervous system.

The study of emergent complex systems, or what we called *emergence* for short, takes the barb out of the advance of scientific knowledge. If immunology is highly dependent on the unique history and features of a given organism, why would we think that the unique features of what it is to be an individual human being will be eliminated by the study of her brain's prefrontal cortex? Complex biological systems produce emergent properties that are unique to those particular systems and interactions. With the myth of full reduction now dispelled, we can study the amazing correlations across systems without worrying that the emergent properties of our conscious experience will turn out to be "nothing but" the firing of neurons, chemical reactions, or "matter in motion."

These are premises we share with Lee Greer, whose critique of Chapter 3 appears above. Because Greer is a careful reader and astute critic, it is our hope that the inclusion of his response will stimulate the sort of productive discussion these essays are intended to foster.

Greer and we agree on several points, especially our shared rejection of certain traditional ways of responding to one of the most powerful of all reasons for rejecting any kind of personalistic theism: the question of why a benevolent God, if such a God exists, would permit the existence of evil. Neither he nor we believe that the classic "free will defense" is sufficient to show that a God possessing the traditionally ascribed attribute of omnipotence is not responsible for evil, and in particular for innocent suffering, in the world. We agree that a God who is able to act miraculously, setting aside natural law in order to bring about good states of affairs that otherwise would not have occurred, or to prevent evil states of affairs that otherwise *would* have occurred, cannot be absolved of responsibility for states of affairs God fails to prevent. We also agree that life has a purpose or at least a meaning, a "calling" higher than selfishness and momentary passions, and we describe the goals of that life in some similar ways.

In the end, however, our views on most of the major questions considered in the third chapter of *The Predicament of Belief* differ rather markedly. For instance, we disagree about both the goal and the results of what is traditionally called "theodicy," the project of "justifying the ways of God" by explaining why God has failed to create or preserve a world in which things like innocent suffering do not occur. We embrace, as he does not, the hypothesis that a not-less-than-personal God is the ultimate source of the natural order and continuously lures living beings toward the good (we call this an "axiological" lure). We argue that, as long as God works within natural regularities rather than setting them aside, God is not culpable for suffering and evil in the world. And we propose, finally, that God can offer this axiological lure without breaking natural law, that is, without performing the kind of miraculous intervention in the world that would compel us to ask why God fails to intervene in other cases.

Greer strongly disagrees. He does not believe that our distinction between divine interventions that break natural laws and a divine "lure" that does not break such laws is a valid distinction; for him, the web of natural causality leaves room for neither form of divine action. But even if a unique divine "lure to the good" existed, Greer believes, it would not help us solve the problem of evil; God would still be responsible for the immensity of suffering in the world.[3]

In one sense, neither of these two disagreements really matters, because Greer does not think that science leaves any room for an axiological lure that originates outside the causal network of the natural world. He challenges two of the major premises of our argument: first, that the human mind is non-nomological (not law-like in its operation) and therefore is open to influences that are not themselves expressions of natural laws; and, similarly, that the universe itself is open to more-than-natural influences. Even if the universe is open in the technical sense that it may not be a thermodynamically closed system, Greer argues, "'the seamlessness of natural causation' means that the universe is causally seamless, such that every effect emerges from efficient causes, where every differentiable symmetry has its corresponding conservation law and vice versa."

Our argument that human thought is non-nomological fails, he claims, for a similar reason. It may be that science cannot predict human actions or explain our thoughts and feelings in neurological terms. Still, science does presuppose "that these phenomena are causally inseparable from and embedded in the physical world." That fact alone, he argues, is sufficient to falsify the "strong emergence" view that we endorse and to invalidate its use as a means of defending any human receptivity to a supposed divine lure.

These are clearly complex issues; it would take a more technical publication than the present one to resolve them. One thing we and Greer do share is the conviction that there are important conceptual connections between how one understands mind or soul on one hand and God's relation to the world on the other. Here (and in the book) we introduce the topic of emergent complexity in recent science because it can assist us in handling both sets of issues.

Put in simple terms, emergence is a position about the nature of evolution. Some people argue that evolution can eventually be explained in terms of the particles and forces studied by physicists. If so, the distinctive feature of living creatures—the agency of organisms in ecosystems—need not appear in scientific explanations of the biosphere. In opposition to this understanding of evolution, defenders of emergence note that vastly different kinds of biological agents and behaviors have arisen over the course of evolutionary history. Emergentists not only emphasize the role of biological agents in influencing the course of evolution; we also claim that agent-based explanations, explanations that reflect the unique features of each organism and ecosystem, are crucial to a full explanation of life on this planet.

Within that broader framework, a series of distinctions has been drawn. Types of agency may vary greatly, or they may be essentially the same; agency may be a new kind of ontological *thing*, or it may be a different way in which matter and energy (as the "real stuff" of the universe) behave; humans alone may be self-conscious and rational, or they may be similar to other animals, just more complex.

One can say that those who affirm the first option in each case affirm "maximal" emergence, while affirming the second option produces a more "minimal" interpretation of emergence. Greer tends toward the minimal end of the spectrum, whereas our view of (say) human nature is more maximalist. Maximalists are sometimes accused of being dualists, though they strongly resist this charge. Minimalists often look and sound like reductive naturalists, a charge that they also deny. As we will argue below, emergence can also play a crucial role in understanding divine activity. That is, we will suggest that the same understanding of emergent phenomena in science that allows us to preserve our sense of ourselves as free, conscious beings also suggests an intriguing way to understand the nature of divine action in the world.

It is in the interpretation of the phenomenon of emergence that Greer and we most fundamentally part ways. Greer affirms an emergentist understanding of evolution—he agrees that evolution produces complex structures whose functioning is not readily explained by a reference to simpler structures and processes—but he rejects the notion that emergence produces ontologically distinct agents who exercise different kinds of causal powers. By contrast, we follow Terrence Deacon in affirming a unique "teleodynamic" (goal-oriented) causation in living organisms, and we defend the role played by mental states themselves in causing other mental states.[4]

Greer sees this position as tending in the direction of (Leibnizian) dualism, and he opts instead for a strict monism that he associates with Spinoza's philosophy. In his view, for example, studying the neural correlates of consciousness requires one to accept that "mental life is inextricably and intrinsically neurological." For over a decade, by contrast, we have been developing a theory of emergent agency that relies not on dualism but on ontological pluralism. Physical forces are real, but so are objects, organisms, and their properties. A vast number of types of organisms manifest countless distinct types of properties. The world around us contains a vast range of (ontologically distinct) types of agency. Ideas are needed to explain other ideas, and all conscious events have neural correlates. But this does not make ideas themselves simply or merely neurological.

Our position allows us to affirm much of what human common sense wants to affirm: dogs are agents in the world, lions have intentions, chimpanzees understand something about the perspectives of other chimpanzees, persons really exist, ideas influence behavior, and it does make a difference that you strive to follow the Golden Rule and live in peace and harmony with your fellow human beings. All these things can be true without standing in the way of rigorous scientific study of humans and the natural world. In short, it's encouraging that there is at least one position on the nature of human thought and action which is neither dualist nor reductionist. Emergence, once again, is the general name for this position (or range of positions).

The Participatory Theory of Divine Action

Probably no issue more troubles those who would believe in God today than the problem of evil. Lee Greer puts it in the form of the famous Tetralemma of Epicurus: "Is God willing to prevent evil, but not able? Then he is not omnipotent. Is he able but not willing? Then he is malevolent. Is God both able and willing? Then how come evil? Is he neither able nor willing? Then why call him God?" But many of us experience the worry about divine neglect in very personal and concrete form: why did my mother have to die such a painful death at a relatively young age? Why would God allow this child to suffer and die in the terrible way she did? Why are whole villages wiped out, without warning, by sudden floods or mudslides?

We agree with Greer on the seriousness of the problem. In *The Predicament of Belief* we did not follow the usual strategy, which is to offer a "theodicy," a defense of God, while leaving most of the traditional beliefs about God and the world unchanged. The problem is deeper and harder than most of the traditional theodicies acknowledge. Unmerited suffering presents a serious predicament for traditional theism, because a God who occasionally steps in to change the natural course of events could eliminate or mitigate such suffering; and God (as traditionally understood) would have every reason to do so. Yet clearly, at a minimum, God very often does not.

The solution to the problem of evil that we offered in the book has two parts. One is the Not Even Once Principle: if God violated the laws of nature even once, God would be responsible for the various cases of unmerited suffering in which God did not respond. We have explained why this is the case in Chapter 3, as well as adding the necessary clarifications and nuances.

The second part of our response is equally essential, though perhaps more difficult to comprehend: the participatory theory of divine action. Imagine that the reader of the Not Even Once argument were to respond, "Okay, I see why God can't be working occasional miracles, setting aside the laws of nature from time to time to reduce suffering. But doesn't that mean that your position lapses into Deism: God may have created the universe but then left it quite literally to its own devices? Whatever theism is, it is surely more than that!"

The objection is a serious one. It led us to consider an understanding of divine action that would not violate the Not Even Once Principle. After all, even a mere act of communication between divine and human minds would seem to violate this principle. For example, imagine that God were occasionally to place clear words into the mind of human beings to save them from suffering or death, such as "Run from the tsunami!" or "Lead your children away from the village; there is about to be a mudslide!" If God occasionally gave some human beings direct information that saved their lives, then God would be responsible for all the times that God remained silent.

One major reason that we are drawn to the participatory theory of divine action is that it does not have this consequence. Participatory theologies affirm that every divine action in the world involves the shared agency of God and at least one finite agent. Larson gives a thorough and insightful description our theory of participation in his comments on Chapter 6. And, as Taylor notes in his comments on Chapter 4, our proposal "allows divine action [we] call 'participatory' because it involved God's acting in and through the agency of finite beings in a manner that did not negate their 'relative autonomy.'"[5] One of the ways God can do this, we suggested, is by acting within us as a continual lure toward the good. (As noted above, we have called this an "axiological lure," invoking the Greek word for value.)

But the participatory theory also turns out to have an important connection to the study of emergent complexity that we mentioned earlier. We saw there that biological agents, acting as agents and not as mere automata, play an irreducible role in influencing ecosystems, and thus in the evolution of the biosphere itself. Similarly, the participatory theory maintains that humans play a role in helping to form the content of divine revelation. We are not merely interpreters of the divine lure; we co-constitute what that message becomes.

The great religious prophets and leaders have often described the divine lure as the call to compassion, to selflessness, and to altruism.

Of course, they have also given some radically different accounts of what God is (if they believed there was a God). According to the participatory theory, this is not merely a matter of conflicting interpretations of a single content—a single set of propositions in the divine mind. Instead, what becomes the content of revelation is in part determined by the constructive activities of human agents. Revelation is a joint product of participatory communication.

Christians have an additional reason to be drawn to this response. As Calvin Thomsen writes in his comments on Chapter 7, on our account participation also lies at the center of the Christ event. Thomsen writes, "What happens...involves a new kind of participatory relationship with the divine reality." Of course, Thomsen also has his reservations about this account:

> If I had been a "participating" disciple in the weeks following Calvary what would I have experienced? What would I have seen or heard? As part of a gathered company of participating disciples, would we all have experienced something similar at the same time and place? How would I know the nature of the link between my participation and the Jesus with whom I had walked the roads of Palestine, fished from the Sea of Galilee, and engaged in earnest conversation over the breaking of bread? How would I experience the call of Jesus to kenotic or self-giving love? The limitation of understanding may be my own—the meaning of the participatory language may be clearer to others than it is to me. (113)

Thomsen presents these questions (which we will take up again for another purpose in Response 2) as, in effect, rhetorical questions, designed to show the implausibility or at least obscurity of our account. But in our view, *these are real questions*. It's more plausible that the testimony that emerged from those days and weeks represented substantial contributions by the original disciples rather than a simple recounting of what happened to them. After all, it is their emerging understanding that has come down to us through the scriptures. Surely the specific factors of their lives—their Jewish beliefs and practices, the context in which they lived, even their language and personalities—played a role in shaping what they came to call Jesus' resurrection.

Nor is the situation different today. We hear echoes in Thomsen's text of Jim Walters' observation in Chapter 8 that "today's inquirers participate in a church community." The range of experiences that we see around us in religious communities surely also characterized the first disciples of Jesus. Should we not conclude that what God has done in the church has *always* been intrinsically linked to what humans have thought and done?[6]

Often the question of divine action is treated as a matter of either/or. Either God directly speaks and acts, or Christianity is a mere human invention. Either God has dictated the words of scripture, which the human authors wrote down word for word, or scripture is a merely human document. Either God works miracles by setting aside natural laws and directly causing outcomes "by His own hand," or there is no divine action. The participatory theory of divine action represents a protest against this either/or thinking. There is a God; God wishes to communicate God's nature to human beings; God continually and distinctively lures each person at each moment. And, at the same time, *what* God communicates is always in part a product of what human agents construe it to be.

For those who struggle with the predicament of religious belief today, there is something very attractive about this response. It does not leave us in a godless universe. It allows us to affirm not only that deeper values underlie the universe, but also that God is actively involved in holding those values before us and calling us to live by the calling that Jesus associated with the Kingdom of God. One can affirm all this without having to believe that God has dictated a specific set of doctrines or ultimate truths that are written down verbatim in one (and only one) of the world's sacred scriptures. We co-constitute, with the divine spirit that lures us toward that Kingdom, what it means to live out the call to compassion in daily life.

Many of us also find that this participatory view matches our sense not only of religious and spiritual experiences but also of daily life. In meditation and prayer, in a worship service, or even on one's daily walk, one senses that a particular act would be a good thing. There is "something of God" in this perception, as the Quakers say; it comes with a sense of a leading. Yet one also recognizes that she must play a role in formulating what this "something" is. Her character, her upbringing and education, and her recent experiences clearly play roles in shaping the God-inspired message that gets spoken and lived. It is not she alone, nor God alone; some combination or fusion of the two agencies brings about new possibilities, new thoughts, new deeds. In short, *both* her own active decision-making and the divine lure are involved. For many of us, it is not hard to believe that the human and the divine interact together in such ways. In any case, in our view, the participatory theory provides a more plausible approach to solving the problem of evil than do the classical views of revelation and divine action.

Having reached this conclusion, we look back and recognize how the earlier discussion of emergence plays an intrinsic role in understanding and defending this position. It has turned out, we believe, that no account of the evolution of life is adequate unless it includes the ways in which organisms have shaped their environments. No "blind law" of evolution determines the outcomes, with biological agents being carried along for the ride. Similarly, God does not act coercively upon human beings, superseding their natural agency. God created a universe built upon deep regularities, so that humans and other animals could come to understand and predict natural phenomena. The Christian tradition has called this process natural revelation. The term is especially appropriate for panentheists, since we believe that God permeates the natural world at all times and that all natural occurrences are in some sense also an expression of the divine energy—what we have called "autonomic divine action."[7]

Special revelation no more supplants human agency than natural revelation does. In this case, we have argued, God is directly luring each person, with content that may be specific to each one. But, for reasons we have described, the content is not pre-established, like words whispered into a person's ear. Human agency is not short-circuited or bypassed; it is completed, made perfect (*teleis*), by the relationship of mutuality with God.

---

[1] Pierre-Simon Laplace, *Essai philosophique sur les probabilités* (1814), available online through The Information Philosopher, http://www.informationphilosopher.com/freedom/laplaces_demon.html, accessed June 29, 2014.

[2] See Richard Dawkins, *The Selfish Gene* (Oxford: Oxford Univ. Press, 2006).

[3] Incidentally, Greer also holds that formulating the problem of evil in terms of the "argument from neglect," as we do, does not capture the full severity of the problem of evil, and that a higher standard for responses (refutation of the charges) must be employed than the standard that we use (plausibility).

[4] See Terrence W. Deacon, *Incomplete Nature: How Mind Emerged from Matter* (New York: W. W. Norton, 2012); see also Deacon, *The Symbolic Species: The Co-evolution of Language and the Brain* (New York: W.W. Norton, 1997). Our program is associated with the school known as "strong emergence"; see Philip Clayton and Paul Davies, eds., *The Re-emergence of Emergence: The Emergentist Hypothesis from Science to Religion* (Oxford: Oxford University Press, 2006); Clayton and Stuart Kauffman, "On Emergence, Agency, and Organization," *Philosophy and Biology* 21 (2006): 501-21. We are also influenced by the "beyond mechanism" movement; see Brian G. Henning and Adam Scarfe, eds., *Beyond Mechanism: Putting Life Back into Biology* (Lanham, MD: Lexington Books, 2013), and John B. Cobb, Jr., ed., *Back to Darwin: A Richer Account of Evolution* (Grand Rapids, MI: William B. Eerdmans, 2008).

[5] See Taylor's critique of chapter 4, citing p. 69 in *Predicament*.

[6] We do not wish to exclude the possibility of God's participatory action vis-a-

vis non-human events and actors. Our position leaves room for divine luring of other organisms. Technically, then, the formulation should read: what God has done in the world, at least insofar as it involves interactions with human beings, has always been linked to what human beings have thought and done.

[7] See Clayton, *God and Contemporary Science* (Edinburgh: Edinburgh University Press and Grand Rapids: Eerdmans, 1998).

10
RESPONSE 2

Christ as "Risen"

In Response 1, we focused on what is in many ways the core hypothesis that emerged from our work on *The Predicament of Belief*: what we are calling a participatory theory of divine action. In fact, we are grateful to all eight of our Loma Linda respondents for helping us appreciate just how important that theory really is, not only to our general account of the possibility of divine action in the world but to our far more specific engagement with Christian claims in particular and even, as we will see in Response 3, to our understanding of the nature and status of religious belief.

Nowhere is the role of participation more crucial than in our discussion over the course of more than two chapters (5, 6, and parts of 7) of what we regard as the most indispensable as well as controversial Christian claim: that a certain ancient rabbi somehow returned to life after his brutal execution by the Roman Imperium, and moreover that his returning to life was in some way brought about by the power of the ultimate reality, which thereby vindicated the rabbi's life and teachings and brought about a radically new relationship between human beings and the divine.

In our engagement with this claim, the participatory theory of divine action plays a double role. In the first place, it poses a significant and, in our view, unanswerable challenge to what is arguably the tradition's standard way of understanding the nature of the alleged "resurrection"— namely, as a miraculous resuscitation, after which the rabbi left his tomb, later to be seen, heard, and touched by his friends and followers. But it also provides a way of understanding the event that, as we argue at some length, not only preserves but in some ways deepens its theological meaning and importance.

In the first section of this part of our response, we will summarize both these aspects of our participatory account of the resurrection. We will then, in the second section, respond directly to the main question our respondents have raised about this account: whether its emphasis on the role of the divine Spirit neglects the importance of embodiment and pushes the resurrection too far in a spiritualistic and therefore dualistic direction. While we feel confident that we can address their concerns, our respondents' comments have helped us see what may be an important way in which our account of the resurrection might be extended and clarified; we will take up that question in the third and final section.

Resurrection as Participation

The negative side of our argument about the resurrection of Jesus— the reason we think a participatory account of divine action, if correct, rules out the traditional miraculous understanding of it—can be stated fairly briefly. According to the participatory theory, God does not act in the world in a way that would disrupt the regularities of natural processes or override the relative autonomy of natural agents. Even in cases where God performs particular actions—for instance, by communicating with beings who are capable of receiving such communication—God only does so in a way that involves and indeed incorporates the responses of those beings in the content of those very actions. That is why, as we write in our chapter on the problem of evil, "every instance of divine-human interaction involves a combination of divine and human contributions" (63). If God were to break the laws of nature by reversing or overriding the natural processes of biological death, what would prevent God, we ask, "from breaking them on other occasions where a far less dramatic miracle would save or restore innocent lives, or at least prevent unnecessary suffering?" (84).

In Chapter 5, we offer an interpretation of the testimony to Jesus' resurrection that once again involves the participatory theory of divine action. On this interpretation, God's "raising" Jesus means God's drawing Jesus' followers into the same relationship with God that Jesus himself had enjoyed. Or, to use our most formal statement of this interpretation in the book, *"in the event that came to be known as Jesus' resurrection, his self-surrendering engagement with God became newly available, through the agency of the divine Spirit, to his followers, then and since, as the form, model, and condition of their own engagement with the divine"* (90). We arrive at this interpretation in part by reading the Gospel accounts of the risen Jesus through the Pauline understanding, developed in the Letter to the Romans, of Jesus' death and resurrection as bringing about the mutual indwelling of the believer and the Spirit (88-89).

In presenting our account in these terms, we risk the misunderstanding that we regard the resurrection either as a subjective event in the minds of the disciples or as a metaphorical way of describing the Christian community per se. So we take some pains to emphasize the divine side of the event—that is, the role of the divine Spirit in drawing Jesus' followers into the same relationship with God that Jesus himself had enjoyed, so that this relationship becomes an *essential* part of divine-human communication, at least for Jesus' followers and perhaps for humanity as a whole. We stress the word "essential" here to prevent the misunderstanding that we think God merely conveys to the disciples an endorsement of Jesus' teachings or presents Jesus as a kind of example as a kind of how they should behave. On our account, the very nature of divine communication with human beings is transformed as a result of God's relationship with Jesus. (More on that later.)

This account of the resurrection leaves some very large questions unanswered. For instance, what should we make of the complex and highly speculative doctrines that emerged over several centuries of reflection on the implications of this event—above all, the doctrines of the Trinity and the Incarnation? In Chapter 6 and again in the latter part of Chapter 7, we explore those questions, ultimately concluding that while acceptance of such doctrines may be rationally *permissible*, they pose conceptual and evidential difficulties that make them very challenging both to interpret and to assess. In Response 3, we will have a bit more to say about what it means to assign varying degrees of justification to the various components of a traditional faith.

There is one question, however, that goes more directly to the heart of our account of the resurrection, a question driven home by both of the respondents who mainly commented on that part of our book: what happens to the traditional insistence that the resurrection of Jesus was (in some sense) bodily?

Resurrection and the Body

Two of our Loma Linda respondents—David Larson and Calvin Thomsen—comment at some length on our account of the resurrection. Both give clear, accurate, and sympathetic accounts of the role of participation in our reconstruction of what occurred in the events following Jesus' execution by Roman authorities (although Thomsen raises an interesting question about the participatory aspect of our account that we noted in Response 1 and will address again in the next section). They share, however, the worry that our spiritual reading of these events—what Larson rightly calls the "pneumatological" character of our interpretation—downplays the significance of physicality or (to use a related but importantly different term) embodiment both in the Christian tradition and in the Jewish conceptual world from which that tradition emerged. Thomsen finds both scientific and theological warrant for affirming the inseparability of mind or spirit and body or physicality, citing current theologians (Nancey Murphy, Warren Brown, and Malcolm Jeeves) who have taken on board the assumptions of contemporary neuroscience:

> In this perspective, "spiritual" factors, at least as they pertain to human beings, have neurobiological correlates. This does not mean that they can be reduced to them, only that they are revealed in them and don't exist without them. In a sense, these contemporary theological writers are pulling the spiritual dimension out of the Platonic sky and back into physical bodies. We do not have a soul tethered to a physical body to be released at death or some other point in the future; we *are* souls. (118-119)

Thomsen acknowledges that our discussion of the human mind in Chapter 3 "sounds very compatible" with the kind of "non-reductionist physicalism" he favors, and the passage just quoted is indeed quite close in letter and spirit to our emergentist understanding of the relationship between consciousness and the brain. But he worries that our conception of the resurrected Jesus departs from that understanding and acquires "a certain kind of dualistic overtone" that moves away both from science and from the biblical texts as interpreted by scholars like N. T. Wright.

Thomsen understands why we stop short of endorsing the traditional view, derived from the Gospel narratives as literally interpreted, that the risen Jesus appeared to certain individuals and groups as a visible, audible, and, in some accounts, tangible physical entity. It comes down, once again, to what we regard as an unanswerable question: if God is willing and able to perform such an extraordinary physical miracle in the case of Jesus, why does God fail to intervene in countless cases in which a far less dramatic miracle would, for instance, prevent appalling cases of innocent suffering?

With that question in mind, Thomsen devotes an interesting section of his essay to a critique of our Not Even Once Principle: that is, as he rightly summarizes it, the principle that God "cannot intervene in some cases of human suffering while failing to intervene in others," because God's intervening even once would create what Thomsen calls "a chain reaction of moral obligation to do the same in countless other cases of human suffering" (6). Now applying the language of moral obligation directly to God may seem a bit anthropomorphic, but Thomsen goes on to fill in the other key component of this argument, which is that "the sort of world that develops rational, moral, and autonomous agents requires a world characterized by regularity, one in which natural laws can be trusted." Either way, it seems that a God who occasionally intervened would be acting in a manner that would be inconsistent with the very nature and purpose of the universe that God appears to have created.

But perhaps, Thomsen suggests, the physical resurrection of Jesus is an exception to that rule: different enough in kind from other miracles that it does not constitute the kind of inconsistency the Not Even Once Principle excludes. He therefore introduces a distinction between "intervention" and "revelation." The former, referring to "ways in which God might alter the normal progression of events to relieve human suffering and improve the quality of life on earth" may indeed be ruled out by our principle. The latter, however, has the purpose of "providing a defining glimpse of an eschatological future in ways that meaningfully shape and define the sorts of lives we are now to live in anticipation of ultimate realization when all things shall be 'on earth as they are in heaven'" (116). What if, Thomsen asks, the resurrection of Christ is "unique, something that happened only once"? What if it is the unique case of what theologians call "'the presence of the future,' or the proleptic experience of the eschaton breaking into human life as we know it"?

In *Predicament,* we explicitly entertained that possibility—the possibility, that is, that the resurrection of Jesus of Nazareth was "a point at which two different 'epochs' overlapped, a point at which two orders or levels of reality intersected"; "an inbreaking of the final reality (or in traditional terminology, the *eschaton*) into the midst of history." We cited the theory among certain theologians (notably Rudolf Bultmann and Wolfhart Pannenberg) that "the end of history somehow became present," commenting:

> [I]f such an event did occur, it could well have been accompanied by effects that would be inconceivable, even impossible, before or afterwards. In that sense, it would not beg the question of why a benevolent God did not act in a similar way on other occasions, even though doing so might have revealed important truths or prevented innocent suffering; such a "kairos" moment (Paul Tillich) would be, by definition, unique. (97-98)

We went on to note, however, that "this hypothesis of a 'boundary event' occurring within the flow of history, though possible, [would] strike some as too far-fetched, or at least too arbitrary, to entertain seriously"; we were therefore seeking less speculative alternatives (98-99). We continue to think that the theory of intersecting or overlapping cosmic epochs provides the best explanatory option for those who remain convinced that Jesus appeared to his disciples in a physical form.

But then the question becomes: is it necessary, theologically or otherwise, to suppose that Jesus in fact appeared to his disciples in that form? Is this necessary even if, for the scientific and theological reasons Thomsen advances, we want to avoid a dualistic separation of spirit and body?

That question is posed in a very searching way by David R. Larson in his response to our Chapter 5. Larson shares our reluctance to regard the resurrection of Jesus as a miracle in the sense of a supernatural intervention—"CK are convincing when they argue that the resurrection of Jesus was wholly natural"—but wonders whether it follows "that for this reason [the resurrection] could not have been bodily. This might have been the result of God working in, with and through what we call nature's 'laws.'" He goes on to provide an amusing account of modern technological advances that "would have been deemed 'unnatural' and therefore 'impossible' for most of human history" (101).

We share Larson's sense that concepts of what is naturally possible are constantly and (in our era) rapidly evolving, and therefore that one cannot in principle rule out a possible future discovery of how a physical resurrection might have occurred without any violation of natural laws. But that hypothesis is no less speculative than the hypothesis of intersecting cosmic epochs. In fact, we know a good deal already about what happens to a human body within minutes of death, and that makes a naturalistic explanation of a physical resurrection uncommonly difficult even in purely speculative terms.

It turns out, however, that Larson is not thinking of bodily resurrection in strictly physical terms. He introduces (as does Thomsen in a slightly different way) the Pauline notion of a "spiritual body" (*soma pneumatikon*, 1 Cor. 15) and then goes on to comment on the various ways in which our pneumatic theory of the resurrection might also involve a notion in embodiment. He considers but (thankfully) dismisses the possibility that we "turn out to be substance dualists after all." Next, he wonders if we think "what the Apostle Paul calls the 'Mind of Christ' is so far advanced that it is substrate-independent or entirely bodiless…" "This alternative," he writes, "would not be substance dualism but a hyper-emergence account and for this reason might be close to their views." The trouble with that option, however, is that "the consequences would be similar to the message of substance dualism: being bodily is dispensable." He then settles on a third option: "This is that for them in the resurrected Jesus the 'Mind of Christ' does depend upon a substrate; however, because of the thoroughgoing transformation that the Apostle Paul describes, this physical or bodily substrate is no longer a human body but the Spirit of God" (104).

Larson's third hypothesis is in fact the right one. We may have made this answer less obvious than it should have been by deferring our account of the nature of Jesus' post-mortem existence until the latter part of Chapter 7, where we explicitly evoke the Pauline conception. In the same paragraph, we also explicitly state the hypothesis that "the personhood of Jesus, after his death, was sustained directly by the Spirit of God." "One function of a physical body," we write, "is to provide the discrete features that identify an individual and that both enable and limit the possibilities of her communication with others." But if we assume that "it is God 'in whom we live and move and have our being' (Acts 17:29)," and if "the mediation of our bodies" is "replaced by the direct agency of the Spirit," then we see "no reason why God could not directly sustain the discrete features of particular persons after their deaths" (131). And there is no obvious reason why a person grounded in a divine "substrate" would count as less fully embodied than a person grounded in a physical one. Hence we suggest, a few paragraphs earlier in the same chapter, that "the Spirit of God itself takes on the role of sustaining the subjective existence of Jesus that Jesus's physical body played during his natural life. Jesus lives, but no longer as a separately embodied individual; instead, as Paul suggests in an especially evocative phrase, Jesus now 'lives to God' (Rom. 6:10)" (129). How, after all, might one better interpret the notion of his now possessing a "spiritual body"?

Suppose, then, that we have successfully addressed the main question that Thomsen and Larson raise about our participatory and spiritual interpretation of the resurrection: namely, whether it is inherently dualistic and therefore hostile to embodiment. We trust we have established that the answer to that question, at least, is no. But this still leaves unanswered a question at which they and other readers have hinted and that we only partially address in the book. We can agree that the risen Jesus "lives to God," in a divinely embodied state that all believers hope ultimately to share. We can also agree, perhaps, that in the events following Jesus' death, his disciples found themselves still or newly able to enjoy the relationship with God to which Jesus had introduced them.

But how do we put those two things together? How do we do justice to the core Christian experience of being in the presence of Jesus and not just of his message, even if the latter is divinely conveyed?

The Spirit of Christ

In *Predicament*, we explore a hypothesis that is designed to explain how Jesus of Nazareth might have been (literally) present to his disciples after his death, even if not in a physically recognizable form. We call it *the personal but nonphysical theory of Jesus' post-mortem presence*, and we make a case for its consistency with the testimony of the earliest witnesses (97-100). But we ultimately back away from it, mainly because, unless one supposes that the presence of Jesus to the small community of his disciples was different in kind from his presence to subsequent believers, it requires one to suppose "that an individual human being, whose cognitive powers and attention one would expect to be less than infinite, can interact with and be personally present to millions of people over hundreds and hundreds of years." Someone who "can hear and respond to the prayers of millions of people at the same time," we suggest, "is a different kind of being altogether from the finite subjects we encounter in the world (101)."

We do consider the way in which the Christian tradition has tried to resolve the paradox of a person who is simultaneously finite and infinite: mainly through the "two natures" Christology (Jesus is simultaneously and inseparably finite and infinite, human and divine) that came to its full realization in the flourishing of Trinitarian theology. Since none of our critics is especially interested in defending Trinitarian orthodoxy, at least in these responses, we will not repeat our reasons for resisting—without fully or definitively rejecting—its attractions (those can be found in *Predicament* on pages 101-4 and again on pages 132-34). For reasons we will address in Response 3, we acknowledge the limits of rational assessments of such claims and the reality that an individual believer may find herself at various times embracing or resisting them—or simply uncertain whether to embrace them or not. But, again: how might we affirm the actual and not just symbolic presence of the risen Jesus if and when we are among those who find themselves unable to follow traditional orthodoxy quite so far?

The question points to an ambiguity in our account, an ambiguity that the present discussion gives us a welcome opportunity to resolve. In *Predicament*, we connect the individual human being Jesus of Nazareth to the resurrection experiences of the disciples (and of subsequent believers) through the agency of the divine Spirit. "But how, exactly," we ask, "is what the Spirit makes present essentially connected to Jesus, and not just a religious ideal or ethical principle that is merely *associated with* the memory of Jesus?"

> The answer must lie in an eschatological dimension: Jesus, after his death, is sustained by God not just as another finite person but as *the* finite subject whose will is most fully and perfectly conformed to the will of God—and for that reason as the "head" of an eschatological community whose members in varying degrees participate in that unity of divine and human will...What the Spirit testifies to, on this account, is the reality of that actual, concrete eschatological community, in which we also are invited to participate. And in making that community present, the Spirit necessarily makes present the reality of the one whose life and unique relationship with God created that community, defines it, and continues to sustain its growth. (110)

The ambiguity here lies in our statement of what the Spirit makes present, or in other words, what God communicates to the disciples and their followers: namely, *the reality* of the risen Jesus. Is "the reality" in this case a living presence that the disciple or believer presently encounters, or is it information *about* a living presence that she hopes one day to join? Is the Spirit giving us Jesus himself, or only pointing to the truth about Jesus' destiny and authority? To adapt some traditional terminology, are we dealing with a real presence or only with a figure that stands for something and someone (ultimately) real?

Thomsen hints at a version of this question when, in a passage we already cited in Response 1, he wonders what it would have meant to be "a 'participating' disciple in the weeks following Calvary." "As part of a gathered company of participating disciples," he asks, "would we all have experienced something similar at the same time and place? How would I know the nature of the link between my participation and the Jesus with whom I had walked the roads of Palestine [etc.]? How would I experience the call of Jesus to kenotic or self-giving love?" (113). Our first response would be that, participation aside, the Gospel narratives provide little help in answering those questions, even if one takes them at face value; recall, for instance, that the disciples on the Road to Emmaus only recognize Jesus "in the breaking of the bread," upon which he instantly vanishes. Even on the assumption that Jesus appears to his disciples in physical form, he is not always easy to recognize!

But Thomsen's questions do lead one to wonder how much specifically Jesuanic content (so to speak) the Spirit would have to include for the disciples to recognize that the experience in question was, in some sense, an experience essentially connected to Jesus himself. There is also the apparently irreducible religious requirement, at least for many Christians, that they regard themselves as in some significant way connected to Jesus and not just to information about him, whatever its source. Both these considerations suggest that we need to go a step further than we did in the book in considering the precise sense in which Jesus of Nazareth was or was not present in the experiences that his followers at some point came to regard as his post-mortem appearances.

The solution may lie in a return to that haunting Pauline statement, already quoted twice above, that the risen Jesus "lives to God." If fleshed out (so to speak) as a concept of spiritual embodiment—again, the Pauline *soma pneumatikon*—along the lines of our discussion in the previous section, it suggests a possible kind and degree of transformation that might enable the risen Jesus to be present in and through the Spirit wherever the Spirit itself is present. The Jesus made present in this way would presumably (and as Paul already suggests) be very and perhaps unimaginably different from the wandering rabbi whose biographical details are now the objects of historical reconstruction, difficult and controversial as that is, given the state of the evidence. But he would have to have enough in common with that wandering rabbi to have enabled at least his earliest disciples to realize that it was the transformed Jesus whom, through the mediation of the Spirit, they were indeed encountering.

In connecting the nature of risen/eschatological existence with the mediating role of the divine Spirit, we are in effect moving between Pauline and Johannine territories. After all, it is the Fourth Gospel that gives the fullest account of the Spirit's role in taking on the relationship with his disciples that Jesus enjoyed during his earthly life. The key text is Jesus' so-called "high priestly prayer"; as we point out in *Predicament*, Jesus in that account "says that after he goes away he will not return to his disciples as the person they knew before his death. Instead, he will send a 'Comforter' or "consoler' (*parakletos*), the Holy Spirit. This Spirit will dwell with and 'in' the disciples and will bear witness or 'testify' to Jesus; he will 'take what is mine and declare it to you' (John 16:14)" (110).

Here, then, is a way in which we might combine the Pauline concept of Jesus' spiritual body with what might be called the Johannine constraint that Jesus' post-mortem presence be mediated through the divine Spirit—and with our participatory theory that the content of divine communication, and in that sense the identity of the divine Spirit itself, has been transformed through the mutually participatory engagement of God and Jesus. We can, and perhaps henceforth should, say that Jesus is indeed literally present to his disciples and their followers—but present now, precisely, as the Spirit of Christ.

11
RESPONSE 3

What Stance Do I Take toward My Own Beliefs?

Our eight critics struggle with the same difficulty that pervades discussions of religious belief in today's world. At some points they argue that our claims on behalf of Christianity are too robust (one simply can't defend Jesus' continuing existence after his death), and at other points they argue that our claims are not robust enough (without the belief that Jesus was physically resurrected, Christian faith cannot survive). Similarly, they struggle with the *mode* of Christian believing. In our scale of six levels of belief (Chapter 7), some of the critics push readers to stay resolutely at the first two and strongest levels, where defenses of core Christian beliefs are claimed to be objectively valid. Others would pull us further along the scale; they ask us to admit that faith is a subjective response to the Christian tradition and that "objectivist" claims are always inappropriate to the nature of faith.

Reflecting on these criticisms has led us to recognize, more fully than we did when we wrote the book, the natural correlations between the "what" and the "how" of belief. It should seem obvious that there would be a correlation between what you affirm and how you affirm it. Yet the nature of this correlation is often overlooked. Reflecting on the connections turns out to be one of the most important steps in finding an adequate response to the predicament of belief as we and our contemporaries experience it.

Some of the connections are obvious. In any field, from physics to political theory, it's true that the bolder your claims, the stronger your case will have to be in order to support them. By contrast, if the question is what you hope will happen or, even easier, why you act as if something were true when you don't actually believe that it is, then subjective reasons will suffice. The degree of difficulty approaches zero when you are not making objective claims at all but just reporting on your personal tastes and desires.

Things become more difficult, however, when it comes to religious faith. The questions our critics have raised have helped us to clarify the position we took in *Predicament*. In what follows we also extend the argument, in at least one major respect, significantly beyond the case made in the book. But let's begin with a brief excursus on the relationship between believing and knowing.

Faith and Knowledge

> But is the core issue really about specific beliefs, specifiable evidence, and counter-evidence? I think not. [Clayton and Knapp] are at the top of their Wittgensteinian game of demonstrating how cold logic can conclude a not-less-than-personal God, given plausible decisions at key junctures in their logic of belief. But this game, helpful as it is to some, misses the point that there is another approach, related but distinguishable, that is more basic and largely missing here—the profoundly religious dimension of reality that exists beyond the evidential game that science plays. (James Walters' critique of Chapter 8, 146)

When one employs reason-based arguments in the effort to escape the present predicament of belief, one always faces the danger of being perceived as *reducing* faith to reason. As its subtitle ("science, philosophy, faith") suggests, *The Predicament of Belief* was written with the conviction that we could avoid reducing the Christian faith to philosophy or apologetics. We believe that religious faith is still possible in this age of science. Since many of our colleagues and peers think that religious faith is problematic, if not downright absurd, we needed to take some time in the book to explain *how* religious faith might still be possible.

To call that exercise a "game" of "cold logic" rather painfully misconstrues the goal of our decades-long work on these questions. *Predicament* is not your standard essay in apologetics; it does not try to demonstrate the truth of Christianity based on "evidence that demands a verdict" (as Josh McDowell so famously put it). In the various chapters we do present the strongest answers we could find to the "predicament of belief" in the twenty-first century. But throughout the book we are equally interested in considering what the various defenses of the Christian tradition are, and are not, able to accomplish. It's worth restating the central conclusions of that evaluative project before we attempt to add something new about what it means to have faith in today's world.

Perhaps our most important discovery is that there are many different ways to defend (or to try to defend) beliefs, and that these different ways fall along a rather clear continuum. The gold standard for rigorous knowledge is quantitative prediction. Solid state physics includes predictions that have been made, and verified, to the level of eight significant digits. (That's like predicting the population of the United States and not missing by a single person.) Believing in God is not the same as believing a particular scientific theory about some part of the natural world. Still, reasons can be given for believing in a not-less-than personal ultimate reality, and the reasons for believing in this reality are stronger (in our view) than the reasons for denying that such a God exists. That, on our view, is about as far as the direct or "objective" arguments go.

At the other end of the spectrum are those who use religious language without claiming that it is true. For some, statements about

God and Christ and resurrection and heaven are false (or more carefully: they have no reason to think that these claims are true and in fact do not believe they are). Still, they say, the Christian language has some positive uses: it raises one's spirits, or adds beauty to life; or it's just how one talks when one is at church, whether one actually believes all of these claims or not. For some, religious language is used as an expression of hope; for others it provides powerful metaphors or inspiring stories.

The Six Stances

We suggest that the distinction introduced above between *what one believes* and *how one believes it* will play a crucial role in helping to resolve these ambiguities about the status of religious language. Applied to the contentious topic of when and how God acts, it will enable us to distinguish—but also to correlate—two questions: what does one actually affirm that God does? And what stance should one take toward each kind of divine action claim, for example the claim that God performs literal miracles in the world?

In *Predicament* we identified six different stances that one can take, which we called "levels" of belief. Some readers have reasonably noted that talk of levels implicitly introduces a hierarchy; it suggests that Level 1 is the highest or best stance to take and Level 6 the lowest or worst. Since we did not intend to rank some of the attitudes above the others, we will speak here of six "stances" that one can take toward theological claims, all of them falling along a single spectrum.

Philosophers calls these stances "epistemic attitudes" or "propositional attitudes." The word "attitude" here does not mean a subjective opinion. Instead, it shows that there are fundamentally different ways in which one can embrace a given claim or proposition. On one end of the spectrum, one can maintain that a given claim is so well justified that all persons should affirm it and, indeed, that it would be irrational not to do so. On the other end, one can conclude that the same claim is not worthy of belief at all; at most one should treat it as a metaphor or useful fiction. Between these endpoints we identify four other stances that a person can take toward a given religious claim.

A concrete example will perhaps make the picture clearer. Consider the claim that Jesus was an important and possibly unique manifestation of the divine. In the book we call this "the Christian proposition" or "PX": that the infinite grace and compassion of the ultimate reality itself were present, and in some sense continue to be present, in a particular human being. Now consider the possible stances one could take toward PX. One could say that PX is clearly worthy of belief, and indeed that the reasons supporting it are so strong that the only rational thing to do is to believe that it's true. At the other extreme, one could say that PX is not worthy of actual belief; the only reasonable response is to deny that it is true and assert that, if one entertains PX, the most one should do is to treat it as a metaphor for something else, or perhaps as a useful fiction. Again, as we will show, at least four other stances lie between these two endpoints.

Like our critics, we are particularly interested in claims about divine action. These claims take many forms: that God guides natural evolution, that God provides inner guidance when we pray, that God works miracles, or that God physically raised Jesus from the dead. Some of our respondents want us to make stronger claims than we do about God's action in the world. Specifically, they want us to affirm that God acts directly ("objectively") in the natural world, independent of the agency of any finite being. Others think that our participatory theory of divine action already asserts too much. Faced with the claims we make in the book, they say, the appropriate stance is *disbelief*: one might hope that our theological claims are true, or treat them as metaphors for something else, but one should not actually believe them.

We disagree with both of these positions. In what follows, we first go through the six stances, exploring the correlations between one what believes and how one believes it. In the course of this exploration, we offer our reasons for affirming or resisting the various stances that theologians and their critics take on toward the question of divine action. We then offer a fuller defense of the position on divine action that we think is most justified—and of the stance that we think it is most appropriate to take regarding these claims.

Direct Divine Action, Known Through Objective Arguments[1]

Stance 1. Some Christians construe claims of divine action in much the same way as one construes scientific theories. For them, PX—once again, the proposition that the infinite grace and compassion of the ultimate reality were present, and in some sense continue to be present, in a particular human being—is something that can be objectively established. When one takes the strongest possible stance toward this claim, one affirms that this is the most reasonable thing to believe.

Well, what would be the strongest possible support that a proposition could have the strongest reason for thinking that it's rational to believe it? We suggest it would be the fact that (virtually) all of the experts in a particular field agree that it is true. These would be claims such as that the speed of light is 186,282 miles per second, or that John Milton was born in 1608. If everyone in the relevant community of experts accepts something as true, or will accept it as soon as they are offered the opportunity, one has a pretty strong reason to think that it's a well-established claim.

Stance 1, in short, represents the gold standard for justification. And it's pretty clear that very few claims in religion—if any—meet this gold standard. In Chapter 2 of *Predicament* we provided what we think is a strong argument for the existence of God. But since this claim is not accepted by virtually every scholar of religion, we can't really take Stance 1 toward our own argument. In fact, it appears, Stance 1 is not really an attitude that one can take toward *any* apologetic arguments in religion, whether they are Christian or Buddhist, whether philosophical or theological.

Stance 2. There is a close neighbor to Stance 1 whose application to religious beliefs is rather more plausible, even though in the end we will argue that it's not an appropriate attitude to take toward most of one's religious beliefs. In this case, one admits that claims about divine action don't exactly meet the gold standard; they aren't claims that win universal agreement from everyone who studies them. But one still believes that one has the objectively better argument, whether or not one's discussion partners concede that fact.

Let's apply this distinction to divine action. If one takes this stance, we argue, one should be able to provide a "theory of error" to explain why one's opponents don't acknowledge the force of one's strong arguments. Imagine that your discussion partners are scientists who believe that God never acts directly in the world. How might you explain their resistance? Your theory of error might allege that scientists arbitrarily limit their domain of study and interest, or that they unfairly exclude some available evidence, or that their naturalistic prejudices close their eyes to facts that they ought to acknowledge. You then conclude that, even if you can't get them to acknowledge your case, you *can* point out why and where they are being irrational. Those who take Stance 2 believe that they can make an objective case for the rationality of their religious beliefs in something like this sense.

Notice what these first two options share in common. Regarding the "how," both take the stance that divine action can be demonstrated through objective arguments. For this reason, when it comes to the "what," they are likely to be defenders of direct divine action. Generally, science supplies the standard for both views, since it functions as an acknowledged standard for objective facts.

An Aside on Intelligent Design

The claim that divine action can be objectively proven is appealing to a broad popular audience of fundamentalists and conservative evangelicals. Book and Bible stores in America are packed with apologetic works that make this assertion, books with titles such as *Evidence that Demands a Verdict* (Josh McDowell) or *The Reason for God: Belief in an Age of Skepticism* (Timothy Keller). Both we and (apparently) our critics in this book find such claims deeply implausible.

This view is influential enough that it deserves a brief aside here. Its advocates rarely limit themselves to PX, since they think that far more can be established. For example, they say, one can show objectively that God sometimes acts directly in history, bring about divinely willed outcomes in the world without needing to rely on the assistance of humans or other finite agents.

The combination of objective reason-giving and the claim for direct divine action—both of which we reject—yields a particular variant of creationism known as Intelligent Design. Intelligent Design is famous for its claim that the idea of an Intelligent Designer beats contemporary science in a head-to-head battle *within the domain of science itself*. Consider, for example, the newest book from Intelligent Design theorist Stephen Meyer, *Darwin's Doubt*.[2] According to Meyer, the rapid diversification of life forms about 530 million years ago, which paleontologists call the Cambrian Explosion, violates core Darwinian rules, for instance the rule that evolution must proceed according to uniform principles ("uniformitarianism"). So, Meyer argues, the best explanation for the rapid development of new life forms is a direct intervention by God. Believing in divine intervention is, *objectively speaking*, more reasonable than believing the standard scientific accounts.

For a host of reasons, we suggest, one should be leery about interpreting the language of divine action as a direct competitor to contemporary science in this sense. In our view, Intelligent Design advocates commit two distinct errors. In Response 1 we already make the case against the position that God directly brings about outcomes in evolution (as required, for example, by Michael Behe's "irreducible complexity"). We have offered the participatory theory as an alternative to direct claims of this sort.

But even if one considers an affirmation that both we and Christian Intelligent Design advocates share, such as PX, we still disagree concerning the stance that one should take toward this claim. Those who regard assertions of divine action as equivalent to scientific claims overestimate the general force of the reasons on which the former depend. We maintain that the reasons for affirming PX are not strong enough that one can put them forward as direct competitors to natural science on the playing field of objective argumentation. Instead, the reasons for affirming propositions of this kind derive from the assumptions and experiences of a particular community or tradition and are not easily evaluated by those who do not share those assumptions or experiences. Hence they cannot compete with natural science on the playing field of objective argumentation.

Divine Action as Hope and Metaphor

Let's move now to the two stances that fall on the other end of the spectrum. Suppose you believe the nature of scientific explanation makes it impossible to give objective reasons for *any* claims on behalf of divine action. Even the non-miraculous divine acts that we have affirmed in *Predicament*, you argue, can only be matters of subjective opinion.

Some who reach this conclusion, of course, are among those who reject religion altogether. But what about persons who hold this view, at least for some periods of their lives, and yet still wish to remain affiliated with their religious community? What kind of stance do they take toward their own religious practice? How do they understand their community's use, and their own use, of the language of divine action? Perhaps, when they speak of God as doing things, they do not mean to make a factual statement of any kind. Perhaps they believe that it's up to science rather than religious belief to determine what counts as fact. They therefore conclude that religious persons like themselves must take a very different stance toward the language that believers use. It seems to us that, if you fall under this description, you probably take one of the following two stances toward your own statements about God's action.

Stance 5. The first possibility is that God-language is used to express a kind of hope: "I hope that human existence is not meaningless in the end," you might say. "I hope that there is a God behind it all who is in some mysterious sense directing human history toward a divine goal." When you read a prayer or sing a hymn that speaks of divine action, you don't actually believe that God is influencing outcomes in the world; and if you don't believe that, you clearly are not claiming to know that God is really controlling the course of history. Instead, your inclination, when you encounter such language, is to treat it as reflecting a hope that you and your religious community share in common. "I hope it will turn out, despite what science seems to demand, that God is somehow working in and through the natural order, bringing meaningful results out of the otherwise random physical events that make up universal history. When I pray for God's providential care, I pray in the guise of hope alone."

In *The Predicament of Belief* we gave this view a more technical expression. Adapting the text (116) to this exposition, we might paraphrase it as follows:

> The individual is attracted to belief in divine action and hopes it will turn out to be true. Perhaps she occasionally finds herself believing in it, but she does not have what she regards as good enough reasons to persist in doing so. If she continues to guide her thoughts and actions by the possibility that God in fact exercises some influence on the world, she does so with the stance of a "seeker," that is, as someone who does not now actually believe in divine action (even if she once did) but as one who hopes that it is true and is attracted to the possibility that she might someday come to believe it.

Let's apply Stance 5 to PX. If this is your position, you can't quite believe that God was actually uniquely present in and through Jesus. Or, if God did do something unique in Jesus, you can't believe that reality is still present today. But, you say, it's not impossible; furthermore, there is something about this possibility that tugs at you, that won't let you go. Whether it's true or false matters. In some part of your being you hope deeply that it's true. You hope for a new world with real divine action and without suffering and injustice—a world with "no more death or mourning or crying or pain, for the old order of things has passed away" (Rev. 21:4). This hope is so strong that it gives direction to orient your life and encourages you to seek community with like-minded people.

Stance 6. There is another stance one can take toward religious claims, a stance still further removed from actual belief. You may hold that the language of divine action serves as a useful fiction (and nothing more). You neither believe that God literally does things in the world, nor would you say that you even have hope-plus-faith that God may have done something unique in and through Jesus. Instead, you use the language of divine action metaphorically. For example, for you "I trust that God will see us through" means "we're going to work very hard to achieve this goal, and I think we're going to make it."

Consequently, when you speak of God's power in Jesus' life, or of Jesus' death and resurrection, you mean that there was indeed something very powerful and valuable in what Jesus reportedly did and taught, and perhaps also in his effect on his followers then and now. It's just that you don't literally believe that God was or is directly causing any of it.

If you take this stance toward Christian language, perhaps prayer for you is a way of focusing your inner energies and strengthening your resolve, so that you can be a more effective actor in the world. Perhaps you greatly value belonging to your particular church congregation, and part of what it means to belong is to use the language your tradition uses. You see no reason why you should have to interpret all of that traditional language in a literal fashion anyway, especially when you know that many of your other co-religionists share your doubts about God's having been uniquely involved in Jesus' life.

As before, we can give a more technical description of this particular stance:

> The individual does not actually believe in divine action, or perhaps believes that statements about God's acts are actually false if understood literally, and therefore does not even *hope* that God is guiding her life or the course of history. But she does think that at least some traditional Christian language can provide valuable metaphors for propositions she regards as true. She may at times allow herself to suspend her disbelief in divine action while participating in religious practices like prayer or worship. If and when this happens, however, she retains at least a tacit awareness that statements about divine action are not true in their own terms but are really, for her, metaphors for something else. (cf. *Predicament,* 117)

Stances 5 and 6 are similar in two key respects. First, in neither case does one actually believe or argue that God directly and independently does things in the world. Nevertheless, both stances allow one still to use traditional Christian language, albeit with a different purpose from those who understand such language literally.

For us, Stances 5 and 6 go too far in the opposite direction from Stances 1 and 2. Just as we found those two stances overly ambitious, we find these two stances overly skeptical. We are not convinced that one has to suspend belief in all claims about divine action, limiting oneself to hope or to metaphor alone. There are (at least) two other stances one can take, and if one adopts one of the remaining two stances, we believe that it's possible to affirm a real divine influence on persons, and thus on the course of human history, without falling into an irrational position.

Divine Action and Subjective Belief

Many of our readers acknowledge strong reasons for doubt, yet they are still drawn to, and often practice, a deep Christian faith. For believers of this kind, we offer a final pair of stances. It's our contention that one or both of these represent the most plausible responses to the core Christian claim about Jesus.

First, a brief recap: persons who take up Stances 1 and 2 maintain that faith can be supported by objective reasons. They tend to affirm direct and therefore miraculous divine acts and to treat them as objective facts. Those who take up Stances 5 and 6 use the language of divine action in either a hopeful or a metaphorical sense. Both ends of the spectrum are popular in the American context today. In fact, the American church often appears to be splintered between just these two groups. The stances in between, by contrast, are less widely acknowledged. Yet they offer a form of belief that is both more interesting (because it is more robust than Stances 5 and 6) and more plausible (because it avoids the overly strong claims of Stances 1 and 2). We suggest that the criticisms raised in the eight critical essays above are best addressed by these two intermediate stances toward Christian claims.

Stance 3. This time let's begin by citing the formulation in *Predicament* before explicating what it means in practice:

> The individual believes that God acts, but she does not expect her belief to be endorsed by scientists or atheistic philosophers. Unlike those who occupy Stance 2, however, she cannot point out any specific mistake that her opponents are making. She therefore regards her beliefs in the activity of God to be irreducibly controversial. Yet given her particular experience and point of view, she has what she regards as good reasons to believe in divine action — reasons she thinks that a neutral discussion partner also should regard as good reasons *for an agent in her position.* This individual, in other words, regards her belief in divine action as rationally indicated, but only for agents who share certain of her assumptions and experiences. (115)

To make the matter more concrete, consider the stronger of the two versions of the "Christian proposition" that we considered in the book, namely the claim that the infinite grace and compassion of the ultimate reality itself were *uniquely* present, and in some sense continue to be present, in Jesus of Nazareth. For many of us, objective arguments don't quite suffice to establish this claim. How can I know that my experiences as a Christian in the twenty-first century are identical or even similar to the experiences of the first disciples? How can I know that they are really experiences of the risen Christ? And on what grounds could I possibly prove that Jesus *uniquely* embodied God's grace and compassion? We don't have good historical records even for the major religious figures in human history, much less for completely unknown saints and gurus whose holiness might possibly have exceeded that of any known spiritual leader in history, Jesus included.

Well, what kinds of experiences *do* serve as reasons for those of us who don't think we have objective evidence but nonetheless find ourselves continuing to believe? Of course, one hears stories of miraculous healings, amazing recoveries from illness, prophetic predictions that later came true. But for many of us, the evidence is rather more ambiguous. We may have had significant, if rare, experiences of the presence of God, moments of divine comfort in times of suffering, even unusual and perhaps life-changing mystical experiences. But experiences of this sort are far from the objective arguments that Stances 1 and 2 presuppose. Nor do they offer a decisive "theory of error," explaining what error atheists are making when they don't believe as we do.

Stance 3 attempts to express the hard-to-define force of these kinds of experiences. They *are* reasons for belief, after all—but often only for those who have had them. When one fails to convince others of the unique power of the revelation of God in Jesus by using arguments, one is tempted to appeal to one's own experiences of transformation that have come through Jesus' life and teaching or through a Christian community. One wants to say, "If you had had the experiences that I have had, you would know what I mean; you would just understand. If you've never had that kind of experience, probably nothing I can say will convince you."

We are advocates of this stance because we believe that this is a rational attitude to take toward one's own religious beliefs—but only if one is honest that her reasons are, in an important sense, personal reasons. They are not accessible to intersubjective verification, although they may well resonate with others who have shared similar experiences and drawn similar inferences from them.

Stance 4. This stance is similar to the previous one, but in this case the subject views her reasons as even more tenuous. Again, we begin with a technical statement of the view:

> The individual believes in divine action but, as in the previous case, does not expect her belief to be endorsed by non-believing scholars, cannot point to a mistake she believes that they are making, and therefore regards her belief as irreducibly controversial. She still has reasons to believe, but now the inferences are complicated enough, the possible criticisms serious enough, and the experiences from which she derives these reasons unclear enough that the status of her belief seems *even to herself* to be ambiguous. So she no longer claims that a neutral observer should regard her reasons as good ones, and she does not regard her belief as rationally indicated, even for an agent with her particular experiences and point of view. Yet she nevertheless has enough reason to believe in divine action that it remains rationally *permissible* for her to do so. (cf. *Predicament* , 115f.)

These two middle positions on the spectrum represent, we believe, the most plausible stances to take regarding claims of divine action, the uniqueness of Jesus, or the resurrection. The difference between them is the difference between claiming that belief in divine action is "rationally indicated (for agents with certain experiences)" on one hand, and only "rationally permissible" on the other. The distinction is not difficult to grasp. In the case of Stance 3, one feels that anyone who has had the experiences that she has had would be justified in believing that God has acted in these ways. But in the case of Stance 4, one maintains only that it is *permissible* for her to believe in these particular claims about Jesus or about God's action—permissible in the sense that one doesn't break any rational obligations when one takes this stance. In this latter case, though, one is not interested in mounting a rational (intersubjective) argument for the claim in question, and she may even feel that she *can't* make such a case. The reasons are real, but for her they are subjective reasons, producing at most a subjective certainty. That's as far as she thinks she can go.

Matching What You Affirm and How You Affirm It

We have seen that no simple generalization describes the relationship between what people believe and how they believe it. Some believe that God acts directly in history but base their belief on subjective reasons. Others deny direct divine action and make an "objective" case for their conclusions in the sense of Stance 2.[3]

But we have also discovered that not just any "what" and "how" go together; sometimes inconsistencies arise. Avoiding the inconsistencies has pointed our discussion more and more in the direction of just two of the six stances toward the core Christian claims. In this final section we will argue that the strongest approaches to divine action avoid knowledge claims that are either implausibly ambitious or unnecessarily humble, while achieving a deep coherence between the "what" and the "how." Stances 3 and 4, alone among the six options, are capable of achieving this balance.

Recall that these are cases where the agent finds herself actually believing claims that she herself regards as inherently controversial. That's what distinguishes these options on one side from Stances 5 and 6 (with which they share the judgment that the claims are inherently controversial, but not the absence of belief) and, on the other side, from Stances 1 and 2 (with which they share the presence of belief, but not the judgment that the claims are inherently controversial). In this final section, we wish to show that an unexpected coherence emerges in these two cases between what one affirms about God's action in the world and how one affirms it.

In *Predicament,* we introduced a fictional believer named Joan to illustrate some of the ways in which beliefs of these intermediate kinds might be motivated; let us reintroduce her here to help us address this related if somewhat different set of issues. Suppose, then, that Joan takes Stance 3 or 4 toward her own Christian beliefs: she really believes them, but she views them as inherently controversial. For the sake of argument, imagine that (like some of our critics above) *what*

Joan believes is that God has acted directly in history. For example, let's say that Joan rejects the "Not Even Once Principle" and maintains instead that God occasionally intervenes directly in the course of human affairs, directly revealing God's wishes through miracles and "divine speech acts."[4] Does she face an inconsistency?

It looks like she does. If Joan really believes that a benevolent God manipulates the course of history in such a way as to bring about specific outcomes, then she also has reason to believe that this God will not permit important truths about divine intentions—above all, divine intentions concerning Jesus the Christ—to go unrecognized by those who would surely benefit from knowing those truths. In other words, Joan's belief in a stronger theory of divine action commits her, whether she likes it or not, to a stronger theory of divine revelation. Her view of the nature of divine action implicitly commits her to the view that God must have been willing to intervene as often as necessary in order to communicate the message that God intends to convey. God's means (direct divine action) should make it possible for believers like Joan to point to evidence of God's intentions. For example, if God miraculously resurrected Jesus' body from the dead, one should try to find evidence that makes it more rational to believe in the resurrection than to doubt it.

But this result clashes with Joan's own stance toward these beliefs! To take Stance 3 is to hold that Christian core beliefs lack strong objective justification and remain inherently controversial. If God *has* acted directly in history by bringing about a bodily resurrection, then when it comes to knowledge of that event, Joan should take Stance 1 or 2 toward these claims. Otherwise she would have to say that God failed in God's communicative intent.

The same constraint holds in the other direction. Assume that you believe that God really influences or "lures" human beings, as in the participatory theory of divine action that we describe above. It would then be inconsistent for you to embrace options 5 and 6, since *these don't involve actual belief in divine action*; they restrict themselves to hope or metaphor.

Only in Stances 3 and 4 does one find the necessary coherence. If God acts only in and through finite agents, as the participatory theory maintains, then it follows that awareness of such action will be available only to those who are themselves participants in that action. Participatory divine action will be invisible, quite understandably, to "neutral" (that is, non-participating) observers. And those who hold up the standards of "objective" argumentation presuppose precisely this stance of neutrality.

This is a very important result, and we are grateful to our critics for catalyzing this unexpected step beyond the text of *Predicament*. Claims about God's directly intervening within the created universe are usually (though not always) accompanied by the assertion of strong objective reasons in defense of these claims, as in the work of the famous Evangelical apologists. Subjective approaches to divine action are usually (though not always) defended in subjective terms, as one frequently finds in more liberal treatments of the subject. (One thinks of Marcus Borg's treatment of Jesus' resurrection in the context of the inner experience of the disciples.[5]) Cases 3 and 4 alone combine a participatory account of *what God does* with a participatory account of *how we know* what God is going.

These pages have led to the discovery of a deep, indissoluble correlation between real belief in inherently controversial Christian claims (the how) and the participatory theory of divine action (the what). This correlation brings a balance and coherence to Stances 3 and 4. Someone who accepts the participatory account of divine action should hold her Christian beliefs in the way these stances describe, and those who are drawn to one of these stances should acknowledge that it is most consistent for them to affirm a participatory account of divine action. In the case of these two approaches to Christian belief, what one believes and how one interprets her own belief are mutually stabilizing, achieving a kind of reflective equilibrium. This fit can be of great value for all those who struggle with the predicament of belief, insofar as it helps us explain to ourselves why we find ourselves taking the kind of stance toward Christian faith that we actually take.

This result is even more interesting when one considers (as we did in the book) that those who find the resting point of their Christian faith in Stance 3 or 4 may occasionally find themselves drifting toward other stances from time to time. On some occasions one may find herself relating to Christian beliefs with other epistemic attitudes. At times of doubt, her belief in (say) Jesus' uniqueness or Jesus' resurrection may waver, and she may respond to that claim with Stance 5 or 6. Conversely, claims that she normally responds to with skepticism or disbelief—say, the claim of a physical resurrection—may become objects of actual belief in particular moments of worship or prayer. Particular Christian claims do not always stay neatly settled into a single category or stance: what one (non-rationally) can't help believing (Stance 4); what one (non-rationally) can't help hoping (Stance 5); and what one (non-rationally) finds oneself imagining and wishing (Stance 6).

This fact—that many today don't settle into a single stance—helps explain still further the attraction of the middle parts of the spectrum of belief. For many of us, it turns out to be impossible to nail down our combination of belief and believing into either a purely objective framework or a purely subjective one. Instead, the vacillations across the stances we experience become part of the natural dynamic of the contemporary life of faith. As we wrote at the end of *Predicament*:

At times, perhaps, the participatory theory will seem to have stopped just short of a vital truth; at other times, the presence of Jesus will slip into the status of something hoped for but not actually believed in. At still other times, the Spirit-centered theory of the resurrection will seem to occupy a reasonable middle ground, since from this vantage point the strongest traditional claims make at least metaphorical sense and the picture of divine action that is least vulnerable to the problem of evil remains intact. (140-41)

---

[1] Note that we use the term "objective" only in epistemological contexts and not as referring to ontological questions of divine action. This usage is consistent with standard practice in philosophy. But it contrasts with some scholars in the theology-and-science discussion. For example, for many years Robert J. Russell has used the expression "objective divine action," subdividing it into interventionist and non- interventionist forms; see for example Russell's *Cosmology: From Alpha to Omega: The Creative Mutual Interaction of Theology and Science* (Minneapolis: Fortress Press, 2008). We find that using the dichotomy of objective and subjective when referring to the ontology of divine action is problematic, in part because it invites the mistaken interpretation that we think divine action is a subjective human creation. It is less misleading to say that the debate concerns the question of whether God carries out some actions that are direct, that is, independent of any participation by finite agents.

[2] Stephen C. Meyer, *Darwin's Doubt: The Explosive Origin of Animal Life and the Case for Intelligent Design* (New York: HarperOne, 2013).

[3] One thinks for example of Richard Dawkins' much discussed but embarrassingly weak case against God's existence in *The God Delusion* (Boston: Houghton Mifflin Co., 2006), or the (more serious) functionalist case against belief in God in the work of some cognitive scientists of religion, such as Pascal Boyer, *Religion Explained: The Evolutionary Origins of Religious Thought* (New York: Basic Books, 2001).

[4] We have in mind Nicholas Wolterstorff, *Divine Discourse: Philosophical Reflections on the Claim that God Speaks* (New York: Cambridge University Press, 1995), a book that we believe falls into the same inconsistency that we are arguing Joan faces.

[5] Marcus J. Borg, *The God We Never Knew: Beyond Dogmatic Religion to a more Authentic Contemporary Faith* (San Francisco, CA: HarperSanFrancisco, 1997); Borg, *Reading the Bible Again for the First Time: Taking the Bible Seriously but not Literally* (San Francisco, CA: HarperSanFrancisco, 2001).

12
EPILOGUE

Seeking Belief and Community in an Age of Doubt

The critical interactions in this volume have helped us advance the argument of *The Predicament of Belief* in some unexpected directions. We have clarified or eliminated some important terms, and we have been led to recognize connections that we did not see at the time of publication. At the same time, the participatory theory of divine action has more clearly emerged as the central contribution of the book. We express our deep gratitude to each of our eight critics for helping to move the discussion forward.

Each of the three preceding sections has highlighted a different facet of the participatory theory of God's action:

In Response 1 we saw *the connection between an emergence theory of mind and a participatory theory of divine action.* Divine-human communication is participatory in a much stronger sense than merely the combination of divine input and human interpretation. The very content of what is communicated by God is shaped essentially by the human response to it. Only for this reason is God able to speak to human beings in a way that preserves their (relative) autonomy. Panentheism, as a theory of the God-world relationship, similarly communicates the combination of human and divine agency that emerges as God works in and through the (relative) autonomy of nature. In both cases, the divine lure is inevitably both divine and natural or human; in fact, that's what makes it a *lure* and not an imposition or intervention.

In Response 2 we highlighted t*he connection between participatory divine action and Christology.* Through his participatory obedience to God, Jesus becomes the paradigmatic instance of participatory divine-human communication. According to this account, the divine will is itself transformed by its participatory engagement with Jesus' freely chosen obedience. Only in this way can one fully see the connection between Jesus' Gethsemane prayer, "not my will, but thine be done," and the high Christological realization of John's gospel, "I and the Father are one." So deep is the participatory relationship in the High Priestly Prayer that the divine Spirit is itself transformed into the Spirit of Christ—the Spirit who is the mode of Jesus' continuing presence to believers.

In Response 3 we emphasized t*he connection between participatory divine action and the believing attitudes that we have labeled the third and fourth stances.* In that response we discovered the indissoluble link between participatory divine action—the God whose revelation culminates in the life, death, and resurrection of Jesus the Christ—and the attitudes toward Christian claims that we described in the book as Levels 3 and 4 and here have described, perhaps more accurately, as Stances 3 and 4. If what is to be believed in is a participatory reality, then it follows rather naturally that one should have access to that reality by participating in it! The kind of knowledge that one acquires through this process can therefore only be a participatory knowledge—a knowledge that combines objective and subjective elements.

Four Implications

We close with four implications that follow from the conclusions reached in these three essays. For the first, note the close parallels between the three central themes that we have addressed: divine action, Christology, and faith. In each case, the relationship is characterized by mutual participation, and in each case it's only through this participation that knowledge is achieved. Divine action starts with God's initiative and is completed only through human response. (Presumably the same holds true for non-human responses as well.) It's not just that God speaks and we as finite hearers distort the message; the message is *co-constituted* by its divine Source and its human reception.

Similarly, the world exists because of God's will and initiative, but *what* it becomes is a joint product of the infinite and finite participants. The scientific story of emergence is the story of progressively more complex creatures co-creating the natural world with God's continual input and lure. One can say that what Christians know as the Spirit of Christ is the "chief exemplification" of this process of mutuality, which expresses the love of God for the world. In the case of Jesus, we believe, an individual person so fully submitted his own created will to the divine lure that the perfect co-participation of God and human could be achieved. Henceforth God's Spirit is present *as* the Spirit of this union, the Spirit of Christ, and Jesus becomes, to use one more hauntingly eloquent Pauline phrase, "the firstborn of all creation" (Rom. 8:29; cf. Col. 1:15, 18).

The second implication concerns the relationship of Christianity to other religions. We argued in the book that the case for the existence of an ultimate reality—the One that Christians call God—is strong enough that this knowledge is in principle available to all agents (Stance 2). But the three kinds of participatory knowledge described in the last two paragraphs above presuppose participation in a particular tradition of religious thought and experience (Stance 3), which means that they are *not* available to "pure" or universal objective reason.

This fact, if such it be, demands of each of us a deep humility in how we approach our religious faith. After all, if there are things that Christians can know only through the practices and experiences of their own tradition, is it not equally conceivable that there may be facets of ultimate reality that are known to members of *other* traditions only through *their* particular forms of practice and experience? At the very least, this is a possibility that we cannot rule out; such is the logic of Stance 3. In other words, the very conclusion that has allowed us to affirm divine action without falling victim to the problem of evil also requires us to acknowledge that members of other traditions may have access to similar kinds of privileged knowledge! There was a day when Christians would have found this acknowledgement troubling. Along with more and more Christians today, however, we find it appropriate, even liberating.[1]

The third implication has to do with the nature of Christian communities. It is no secret that traditional churches are losing members in Europe and North America, and that many new kinds of Christian communities are springing up.[2] We begin to describe the church of the future in Chapter 8, and we are grateful to Jim Walters for extending our reflections even further in his chapter above. This theme is so large, and so important, that it will be the central theme of our next book. There we will ask, among other questions, whether the current priority of Christians in America should be defending and strengthening existing denominations or building a movement that is independent of denominational and even of confessional allegiances.

We wish to close this book by noting one final implication of these chapters. It concerns a vital question for Christian identity and piety, first raised in our second response: to what extent can Christians who embrace our position regard themselves as in some significant way connected to Jesus and not just to information about him? We want to make sure that the complexities of our answer do not obscure the heart of our response, which is that *the risen Jesus can be present in and through the Spirit wherever the Spirit itself is present.* Just as, through the outpouring of the Holy Spirit at Pentecost, the first disciples encountered a transformed version of the Jesus whom they had known in the flesh, so also Christians today encounter through the same Holy Spirit, the Spirit of Christ, the Jesus whom they also know through the Gospels.

It is the job of the theologian to provide a sophisticated interpretation of the basic elements of the Christian faith. But the complexities of the debates often obscure the simple truths that theologians seek to convey. When we write (in Response 2 above) that "Jesus' post-mortem presence [is] mediated through the divine Spirit," we mean readers to hear echoes of Jesus' words in the High Priestly prayer (John 14-17). When we write that "Jesus is indeed literally present to his disciples and their followers—but present now, precisely, as the Spirit of Christ," we mean to convey the content of countless liturgies, hymns, and prayers.

Addressing the complexities of Christian belief in the twenty-first century is no easy task, and we do not want to minimize the costs of finding a genuinely adequate solution. Still, perhaps the most surprising part of our twenty-five-year attempt to address "the predicament of belief" is how many of the core beliefs of the Christian tradition as it arose so many centuries ago can still be affirmed in the vastly different context in which we live today.

[1] Brian D. McLaren, *Why Did Jesus, Moses, the Buddha, and Mohammed Cross the Road? Christian Identity in a Multi-faith World* (New York: Jericho Books, 2012).
[2] For a new nation-wide "network of networks" of these new kinds of community, see www.CanaInitiative.org.

CONTRIBUTORS

William Breer is a forensic psychotherapist whose graduate degree is in social work. After years of atheism and searching world religions, he turned to Roman Catholicism and is a lay member of the Benedictine Order, Saint Andrew's Monastery, Palmdale, California, where he is working on issues in spiritual direction and psychotherapy. He is published in his field and has written scores of psychological reports for the California court system.

Philip Clayton is Ingraham Professor at the Claremont School of Theology and the author or editor of some twenty books and close to 200 articles in philosophy, theology and the religion-science debate. In recent years, Clayton has focused increasingly on the rapidly changing context for religious belief and practice in North America and around the world. He is currently working with the Convergence Network on emerging forms of Christian community and on revitalization efforts in congregations, denominations, and seminaries.

Lee F. Greer is an associate project scientist at the University of California, Irvine, researching the genomics and demographics of aging and collaborating on papers and book chapters. He is an evolutionary biologist with graduate degrees in biology, including a doctorate from Loma Linda University. He has published on aging, systematics, and is collaborating on studies of ancient human DNA. He plays guitar, enjoys the outdoors, the history of ideas in science, philosophy, and religion, and social and environmental activism. Lee lives in Riverside, California with his wife and their three children.

Dennis Hokama, a lay theologian who did graduate work in the behavioral sciences, analytically studies science, the Bible, and Adventist history. Born of missionary parents, he grew up in Japan, but has mostly lived in Los Angeles and worked as a personnel analyst and resource specialist teaching English and math. He has published in *Adventist Today* and *Adventist Currents*, and written over a hundred unpublished essays. When he isn't reading in the historical-critical study of Scripture or probability theory, he may be found playing a mean game of chess.

Steven Knapp is the sixteenth president of the George Washington University, Washington, DC, where he is also a professor of English. He is the author of two books and author or coauthor of numerous articles and lectures on literature, literary theory, philosophy and religion. He earlier served as dean of arts and sciences and then as provost at the Johns Hopkins University; before that, he taught at the University of California at Berkeley, where his courses focused on the works of John Milton, English Romanticism, literary theory, and the Bible as literature.

David R. Larson teaches in the Loma Linda University School of Religion where he co-founded and led its Center for Christian Bioethics for many years. A graduate of Pacific Union College, Claremont School of Theology and Claremont Graduate University, he specializes in theological, biomedical and sexual ethics. He has published and posted on the Internet many articles, chapters and reviews and is the editor of *Abortion: Ethical Issues and Options*. (1992). Along with Fritz Guy and David Ferguson, he is also a co-editor of *Christianity and Homosexuality: Some Seventh-day Adventist Perspectives* (2008).

Richard Rice is a philosophical theologian, with graduate degrees from Andrews University and the University of Chicago Divinity School. He has served in pastoral ministry and is now a religion professor at LLU. His areas of particular interest are the doctrine of God and the theology of suffering. He has written nearly a hundred articles and seven books, including *God's Foreknowledge and Man's Free Will* (1985) and *Suffering and the Search for Meaning: Contemporary Responses to the Problem of Pain* (2014). He and his wife Gail enjoy traveling and spending time with their children and grandchildren.

Christopher Southgate serves as Principal of the training course for Anglican ordinands in the South West of England, and is also Senior Lecturer in Theology at the University of Exeter. He has published extensively on the problem of suffering in evolution and is the editor of the science-religion textbook *God, Humanity and the Cosmos*, now in its third edition (Continuum 2011). He also writes on ecotheology, as in the co-authored monograph *Greening Paul* (Baylor 2010). His other activity is as a poet, and of his six collections the latest is *A Gash in the Darkness* (Shoestring 2012).

Ervin Taylor is an archaeologist specializing in geochronology. He received his PhD at UCLA in anthropology with an emphasis in archaeology. He is now Professor Emeritus at UCR, a Visiting Professor in the Cotsen Institute of Archaeology, UCLA, and Visiting Scientist at the Accelerator Mass Spectrometry Laboratory, UCI. Twenty years ago, he co-founded *Adventist Today* and served for a decade as executive publisher. He and his wife live in Loma Linda, California and enjoy two grown children and four grandchildren.

Calvin Thomsen is a pastoral theologian, whose career has been primarily in large Southern California pastorates, but who has recently joined LLU's School of Religion after completing his PhD in marital and family therapy at LLU's School of Behavioral Science. He earlier earned professional degrees in religion at Andrews University and Fuller Theological Seminary. Thomsen's particular research interest is neuroscience and religion, and for relaxation he enjoys playing the piano and guitar as well as backpacking and snow skiing.

James W. Walters is a theological ethicist at Loma Linda University, and did graduate work at Andrews University, the Anabaptist Mennonite Biblical Seminary, and Claremont Graduate University. He has been a professor for 35 years, pastored churches, and co-founded *Adventist Today* and LLU's Center for Christian Bioethics. He has published a half-dozen books and scores of articles, and won grants from the NEH and NIH. He likes hiking the High Sierra, and he and wife Priscilla have two daughters and one granddaughter.

www.ingramcontent.com/pod-product-compliance
Lightning Source LLC
Chambersburg PA
CBHW070312230426
43663CB00011B/2101